THE BEST IN TENT CAMPING:

VIRGINIA

A Guide for Campers Who Hate RVs, Concrete Slabs, and Loud Portable Stereos

THE BEST IN TENT CAMPING:

VIRGINIA

A Guide for Campers Who Hate RVs, Concrete Slabs, and Loud Portable Stereos

Randy Porter

Menasha
Ridge Press

Printed in the United States of America
Published by Menasha Ridge Press
First Edition, first printing

Distributed by The Globe Pequot Press

Library of Congress Cataloging-in-Publication Data

The best in tent camping, Virginia : a guide for campers who hate RVs, concrete slabs, and loud portable stereos
p. cm.
Includes bibliographical references (p. 169)
ISBN 0-89732-316-5 (pbk.)
1. Camp sites, facilities, etc.—Virginia—Guidebooks.
2. Camping—Virginia—Guidebooks. 4. Virginia—Guidebooks.
I. Title.
GV191.42.V8 P67 2000
796.54'09755—dc21

00-056120
CIP

Cover design by Grant Tatum

Menasha Ridge Press
P.O. Box 43673
Birmingham, Alabama 35243
www.menasharidge.com

CONTENTS

MAP LEGEND

WHITE WOLF Campground name and location	Table Rock Other nearby campgrounds	NATIONAL FOREST / NATIONAL PARK Public lands	N 0 1 2 MILES Approximate scale
64 Interstate highways	40 U.S. highways	120 49 State roads	22 Other paved roads
Unpaved roads	4WD Jeep roads	FS 80 CR 80 U.S. Forest Service and County roads	Railroads
Asheville City or town	Ward Lake Ocean, lake, or bay	Swift Creek River or stream	Political boundary

Bridge or tunnel	Lighthouse	Park office
Cliff or outcropping	Lodging	Picnic area
Falls or rapid	Marina or boat ramp	Spring
Food	Mine or quarry	Stable or ranch
Historical site	Museum	3312 Summit or lookout
House or cabin	Observatory	
	ORV area	

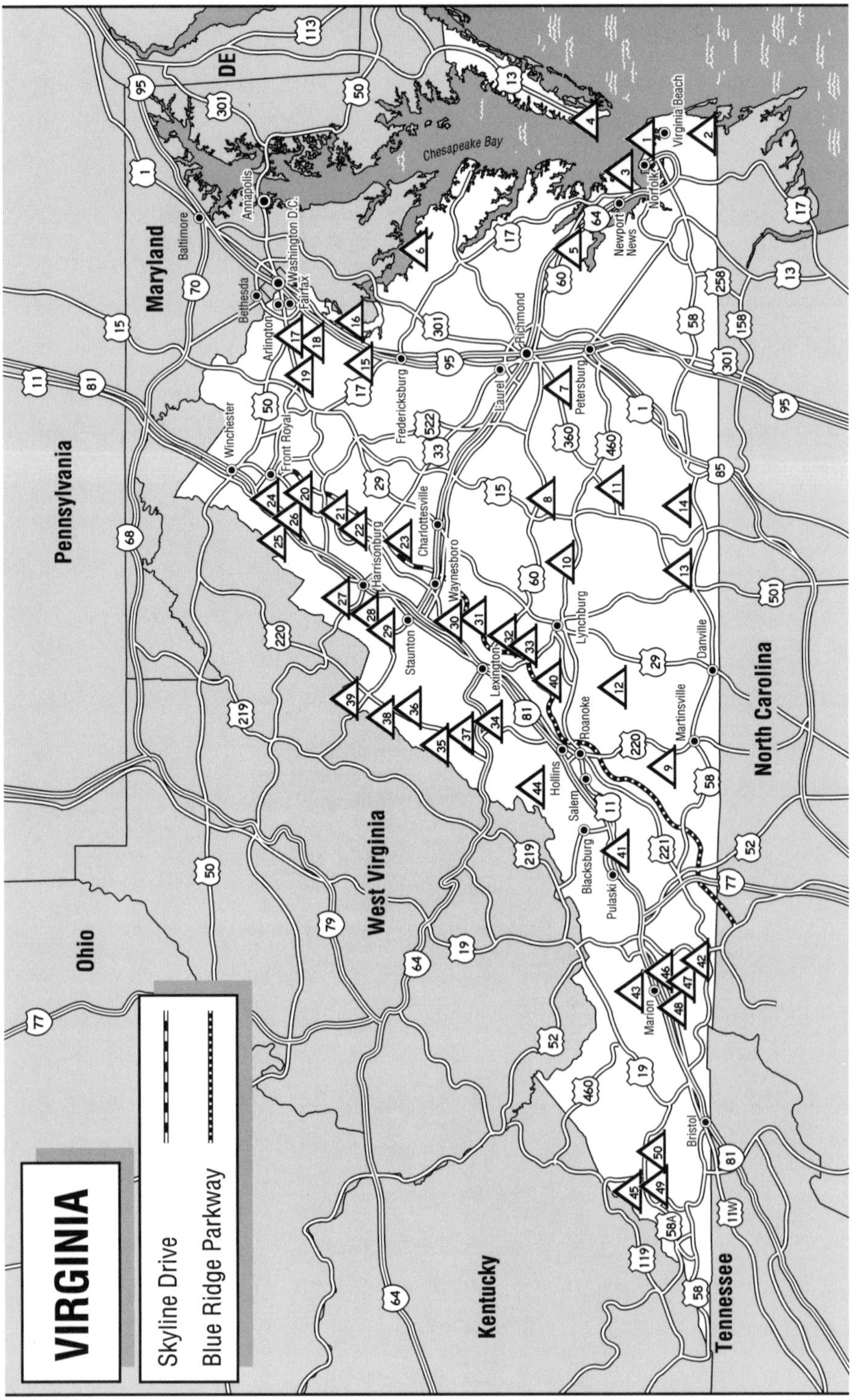
VIRGINIA
Skyline Drive
Blue Ridge Parkway
Pennsylvania
Maryland
DE
Ohio
West Virginia
Kentucky
Tennessee
North Carolina
Chesapeake Bay
Baltimore
Annapolis
Washington D.C.
Bethesda
Arlington
Fairfax
Winchester
Front Royal
Fredericksburg
Harrisonburg
Charlottesville
Waynesboro
Staunton
Lexington
Lynchburg
Richmond
Laurel
Petersburg
Newport News
Norfolk
Virginia Beach
Roanoke
Hollins
Salem
Blacksburg
Pulaski
Marion
Bristol
Martinsville
Danville

PREFACE

Virginia is a state, actually a commonwealth, whose history and natural beauty are best described in superlatives. Her scenery varies from the coastal plain along the Atlantic Ocean and Chesapeake Bay to mountain ranges in the west and southwest. Her history parallels that of the New World, with the first settlers arriving in 1607, more U.S. presidents coming from Virginia than any other state, and the majority of Civil War battles being fought here. While the country was mired in the Great Depression in the 1930s, Virginia's public lands were the fortunate recipients of much of the labor of the Civilian Conservation Corps. As you travel about through the Old Dominion's federal- and state-managed public lands, you'll swim in lakes, hike on trails, and pitch your tent in areas that were born of one of the country's darkest periods.

I've lived in Virginia and explored its wooded countryside for three decades, and I still find myself overwhelmed by her glorious landscape and central role in the birth and growth of the United States. There's no better way to get to know the Old Dominion than by pitching a tent and camping out up close and personal. Walk her trails, fish in her streams, and sleep under her stars; and I'm convinced that you, too, will be taken by her charms.

—Randy Porter

INTRODUCTION

A Word about this Book and Virginia Camping

Virginia's history, varied topography, and natural features are rivaled by few other states. As I crisscrossed its length and breadth, I never ceased to be fascinated by those attributes. Just as varied are the places to camp. Some parts of the state have changed little since the country's first settlers stepped ashore in 1607 and others would be unrecognizable by John Smith and his fellows. For that matter, some areas appeared foreign to me when I revisited a year or so later.

As you travel about with *The Best in Tent Camping: Virginia* in hand, I know that you too will be mesmerized by a state whose camping areas vary so markedly from one another. From the coast to the tops of mountains, and from large urban areas to the great beyond, I found a lot of really neat places to pitch a tent for a night or longer. If there were but 50 campgrounds in the entire Old Dominion, as the Commonwealth of Virginia is often called, my task would have been much simpler. But I found vast differences, from municipal campgrounds in northern Virginia to primitive ones in the national forests. No excuses, no apologies—that's just the way it is. Baskin-Robbins has 33 flavors, and depending on where you choose to sleep, you may find yourself next to a golf course or you may find nary a pit toilet.

The question then arises, what's camping all about if so many different sites can fall under one title? Is it finding wilderness among a population center of 3,000,000 people or is it looking into the flames of a fire that's miles from the nearest person? I'm not sure that one definition fits all, nor would I be comfortable with an exclusionary policy that would rule out some and include others based on an arbitrary concern. In the course of using this book to explore Virginia's campgrounds, you may very well come across a concrete slab, a loud radio, and even an RV or two.

Ultimately, camping is not about the size of your tent, or the distance from the next site, or even what sanitary facilities are there, although those things are definitely good to know. It's about the mindset that you bring to the outdoors and the one you've left at home. But this I guarantee—if you embark into the outdoors with an open mind and a spirit of adventure, wherever you go, you'll find yourself at home in the woods. You'll learn a little about your surroundings, and a lot about yourself.

The rating system

Within the scope of the campground criteria for this book—accessible by car and preferably not by RV, scenic, and as close to a wilderness setting as possible—each campground offers its own characteristics. The best way to deal with these varying attributes was to devise a rating system that highlights each campground's best features. On our five-star ranking system, five is the highest rating and one is the lowest. So if you're looking for a campground that is beautiful and achingly quiet, look for five stars in both of those categories. If you're more interested in a campground that has excellent security and cavernous campsites, look for five stars in the Site Spaciousness and Security categories. Keep in mind that these ratings are based somewhat on the subjective views of the author and her sources.

Beauty

If this category needs explanation at all, it is simply to say that the true beauty of a campground is not always what you can see but what you can't see. Or hear. Like a freeway. Or roaring motorboats. Or the crack, pop, pop, boom of a rifle range. An equally important factor for me on the beauty scale is the condition of the campground itself and to what extent it has been left in its natural state. Beauty also, of course, takes into consideration any fabulous views of mountains, water, or other natural phenomena.

Site privacy

No one who enjoys the simplicity of tent camping wants to be walled in on all sides by RVs the size of tractor trailers. This category goes hand in hand with the previous one because part of the beauty of a campsite has to do with the privacy of its surroundings. If you've ever crawled out of your tent to embrace a stunning summer morning in your skivvies and found several pairs of very curious eyes staring at you from the neighbor's picture window, you'll know what I mean. I look for campsites that are graciously spaced with lots of heavy foliage in between. You usually have to drive a little deeper into the campground complex for these.

Site spaciousness

This is the category you toss the coin on—and keep your fingers crossed. I'm not as much of a stickler for this category because I'm happy if there's room to park the car off the main campground road, enough space to pitch a two- or four-man tent in a reasonably flat and dry spot, a picnic table for meal preparation, and a fire pit safely away from the tenting area. At most campgrounds, site spaciousness is sacrificed for site privacy and vice versa. Sometimes you get extremely lucky and have both. Don't be greedy.

Quiet

Again, this category goes along with the beauty of a place. When I go camping, I want to hear the sounds of nature. You know, birds chirping, the wind sighing, a surf crashing, a brook babbling. That kind of stuff. It's not always possible to control the noise volume of your fellow campers, so the closer you can get to natural sounds that can drown them out, the better. Actually, when you have a chance to listen to the quiet of nature, you'll find that it is really rather noisy. But what a lovely cacophony!

Security

Quite a few of the campgrounds in this book are in remote and primitive places without on-site security patrol. In essence, you're on your own. Common sense is a great asset in these cases. Don't leave expensive outdoor gear or valuable camera equipment lying around your campsite or even within view inside your car. If you are at a hosted site, you may feel more comfortable leaving any valuables with them. Or let them know you'll be gone for an extended period so they can keep an eye on your things.

Unfortunately, even in lightly camped areas, vandalism is a common camping problem. In many places, the wild animals can do as much damage as a human being. If you leave food inside your tent or around the campsite, don't be surprised if things look slightly ransacked when you return. The most frequent visitors to food-strewn campsites are birds, squirrels, chipmunks, deer, and bears.

Cleanliness/upkeep

By and large, all the campgrounds in this book rank five stars for this category. I think Washington and Oregon campgrounds are some of the cleanest and tidiest spots I've been in due to the fine management of park and Forest Service attendants. The only time they tend to fall a bit short of expectation is on busy summer weekends. This is usually only in the larger, more developed compounds. In more remote areas, the level of cleanliness is most often dependent on the good habits of the campers themselves. Keep that in mind wherever you camp.

CAMPGROUNDS ON THE COAST

FIRST LANDING STATE PARK

Virginia Beach

Seashore State Park joined five other state parks as the first to be launched into the fledgling system on June 15, 1936, and was renamed First Landing State Park in 1999. While much is known about the role of Jamestown in the settlement of the New World, the park's new name reflects the lesser-known fact that the Virginia Company landed first at this site on the Chesapeake Bay on April 26, 1607, before proceeding to and landing at Jamestown on May 13. Among First Landing's current distinctions: it's the most visited park in Virginia's system with more than 1.2 million visitors annually. Perhaps First Landing's greatest draw is its proximity to all of the activity that one might expect in Virginia Beach, the largest city in Virginia and deemed the world's largest resort city. However, for myself and many other campers who crave solitude when we pitch a tent, the park's popularity and location in a city of approximately 430,000 people are also its biggest detractors.

Shore Drive, also US 60, divides First Landing's campground and its trail system and day-use area, so traffic through the campground is limited to campers and their vehicles. In addition, the beachfront swimming area is open only to campers, so don't let those 1.2 million visitors keep you from spending the night here. Two large loops fan out to the right and left of the campground entrance station for access to

CAMPGROUND RATINGS

Beauty: ★★★
Site privacy: ★★
Site spaciousness: ★★★
Quiet: ★★
Security: ★★
Cleanliness/upkeep: ★

The park's new name reflects the lesser-known fact that the Virginia Company landed first at this site on the Chesapeake Bay on April 26, 1607, before proceeding to and landing at Jamestown on May 13.

COASTAL

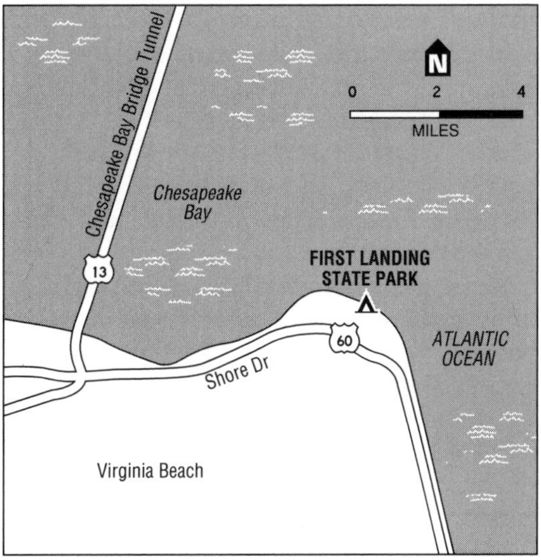

the 222 sites, which are separated by small sand dunes and trees. Tent campers are not allowed on the beachside sites, but it's just a short walk from most sites to the beach via well-placed boardwalks across the dunes.

First Landing's trails can be accessed from the visitor center on the opposite side of US 60 from the campground. The six-mile (point-to-point) Cape Henry Trail is extremely popular among bicyclists and stays very busy, especially on weekends during the summer. Those out for a nice walk should keep that in mind and stick to the 19 miles of alternate trails that restrict bicycles and range from the 0.3-mile Fox Run Trail to the 5-mile Long Creek Trail. Besides the usual coastal landscape that you might expect to find here where the Atlantic Ocean meets the Chesapeake Bay, the park is the northernmost location on the East Coast where you can see both subtropical and temperate plants growing together, which is why it was included in the National Register of Natural Landmarks in 1965. As you walk through sand dunes that reach as high as 75 feet, don't be surprised to see Spanish moss hanging from bald cypress, wild olive, live oak, and beech trees. You're bound to encounter different varieties of scenery and vegetation depending on the trail you choose.

Described as the park's most popular trail, the 1.5-mile Bald Cypress Loop Trail starts from the visitor center and will take you along boardwalks through cypress swamps complete with resident pileated woodpeckers and turtles sunning themselves on logs. The Long Creek Trail starts at the main park, beginning on the park's main road, and will lead you through salt marshes where you'll see osprey nests and great blue herons and egrets stalking their prey. As is the case in any low-lying camping area, be sure to bring an ample supply of bug spray.

I would be remiss if I didn't mention False Cape State Park located just a few miles away in the community of Sandbridge. False Cape's ranking as the least visited park in the state system can be attributed to its limited access restricted to bicycle, boat, foot, and now, an electric tram. However, the opportunity to explore this near-pristine barrier peninsula and share the experience with few other visitors puts it at the top of my list within Virginia's state park system. If you're similarly inclined to leave the crowds behind, a day trip to False Cape is a must.

Because of First Landing's popularity, camping here can end up being an inexpensive way to stay at this bustling resort city rather than an opportunity to get away from your own particular rat race. You'll find it easiest to enjoy the pleasures and natural beauty that First Landing State Park has to offer if you can schedule your visit during the week or outside of the busy summer months.

To get there: From I-64, take exit 282 heading north on US 13. After approximately eight traffic lights, turn right onto US 60/Shore Drive, the last exit before the Chesapeake Bay Bridge Tunnel. Go 4.5 miles to the park's entrance.

KEY INFORMATION

First Landing State Park
2500 Shore Drive
Virginia Beach, VA 23451

Operated by: Virginia Department of Conservation and Recreation

Information: (757) 412-2300

Open: First weekend in March–December 1

Individual sites: 222

Each site has: Picnic table, fire ring, and lantern pole

Site assignment: Campers can choose from available sites

Registration: By phone, (800) 933-PARK; or at campground on arrival. Advance registration is highly recommended due to the popularity of this campground.

Facilities: Water, hot showers, laundry, camp store, and pay telephone

Parking: At campsite

Fee: $18 per night

Elevation: Sea level

Restrictions:

Pets—On leash or in enclosed area and not allowed in swimming areas or toilet facilities

Fires—In fire rings, stoves, or grills only

Alcoholic beverages—Prohibited

Vehicles—Park in marked areas only

Other—Do not damage any live trees; hiking trails are for walkers only; bicycles only on park roads and the Cape Henry Trail; no motorized vehicles on trails; 14 of 30 days maximum stay

NORTHWEST RIVER PARK

Chesapeake

Northwest River Park's 763 acres lie near the southern border of Virginia on the coastal plain. Those coming for the day or to spend a few nights are sure to find the peace and quiet they're looking for with Indian Creek, Northwest River, and Smith Creek surrounding the park on three sides and a 29-acre lake meandering through the middle of it. But don't worry about arriving unprepared to enjoy the water because paddle boats, jon boats, and canoes are all available for rent. You may also enjoy fishing in the stocked freshwater lake for bass, bluegill, crappie, catfish, and trout. The land was formerly cultivated farmland, although shadier activities also went on here. Over 30 sites for making moonshine have been found on the property, including 4 in the area known as Moonshine Meadow.

Entering the park off Indian Creek Road, you'll arrive at the six-sided camp store and office next to the lake and boat rental area. Across the gravel road is the miniature golf course. After registering, take the gravel road to the right to reach the campground. The campground consists of 72 sites set out on two loops among a grove of towering oaks. The area is flat and shaded with little vegetative barrier between sites. They are spacious, however, and well separated from each other. Of the 21 tent sites (those without electric hookups), the most popular and private ones are 52, 53, 55, 58,

CAMPGROUND RATINGS

Beauty: ★★★
Site privacy: ★★★
Site spaciousness: ★★★
Quiet: ★★★
Security: ★★★
Cleanliness/upkeep: ★★★★

The land was formerly cultivated farmland, although shadier activities also went on here.

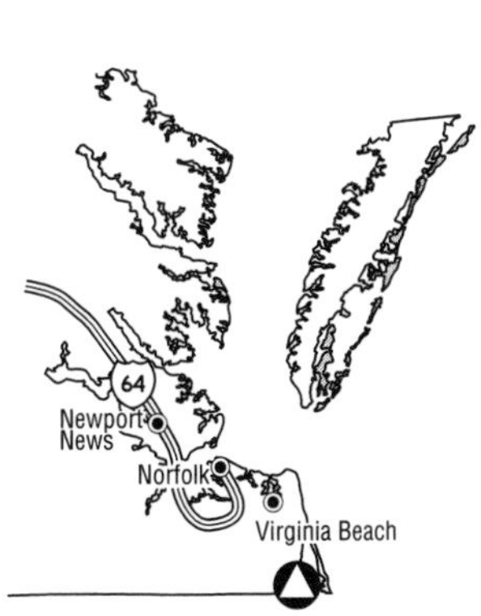

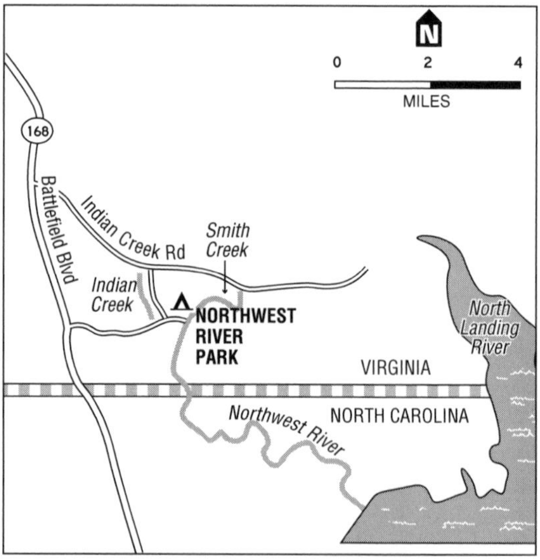

59, 61, 63, 65, 67, 68, and 70, which lie on the campground's outer edge. A backdrop of bamboo and hardwoods shield these sites but can also stifle breezes wafting through the campground. This is an important consideration when camping in a low-lying and potentially very buggy area. It's strongly suggested that you pack an ample supply of bug spray.

Those looking for longer adventures on the water should not feel confined to the park's boundaries. From the confluence of Indian Creek and Northwest River at Otter Point, it's just a couple of miles to the North Carolina border. In addition to paddling through the lazy waters that surround the park, there are other activities for outdoors folk. The trails at Northwest River Park offer a chance to view the swampy topography up close. Its environment is home to wood ducks and river otters, as well as marsh vegetation such as water tupelo, bald cypress, mistletoe, and Christmas fern. Trails range in length from the 0.75-mile Deer Island Trail to the 2.5-mile Indian Creek Trail. The Deer Island Trail is accessible near the campground entrance and the Shuttle Road where several of the other trails also emerge. Along the Indian Creek Trail you'll find the arched hickory tree and resurrection fern, which turns brown when dry and then greens up nicely when it rains. The 1.5-mile Molly Mitchell Trail located on the northeastern corner of the park was named in honor of former landowners who lived where the group picnic shelter now stands. The Scenic Slough provides excellent habitat for wood ducks, otters, squirrels, reptiles, and amphibians. The one-mile Otter Point Trail can be found on the southern edge of Northwest River

Park. Among the park's bald cypress trees, there is one towering specimen that has a large towering base and is thought to be several hundred years old.

Bikes are not allowed on the trails but are a nice way to get around on the park's sandy roads. Should you bring your two-wheeler, be sure to pedal along the Shuttle Road out to Otter Point. This grassy open area offers a great spot for picnics, dropping a fishing line, or communing with nature at the confluence of Indian Creek, Smith Creek, and the Northwest River. A curious "trail" is the short, but winding, boardwalk loop around the fragrance garden for those who are visually impaired or just enjoy a sweet-smelling garden. It's located next to the camp store. All of the park's trails are well marked and well maintained.

In addition to those activities that can be done on your own, park staff will accompany groups of ten or more on canoe trips as well as provide paddling instruction. Turning your gaze skyward, you can learn more about the heavens with the Backbay Amateur Astronomers, who meet in the evenings at the Equestrian Area.

To get there: From I-64, take the Battlefield Boulevard exit (Rt. 168) heading south. Continue 15 miles and turn left onto Indian Creek Road. Go 4 miles to the campground entrance.

KEY INFORMATION

Northwest River Park
1733 Indian Creek Road
Chesapeake, VA 23322

Operated by: City of Chesapeake Parks and Recreation Department

Information: (757) 421-7151/3145

Open: April 1–December 1

Individual sites: 72

Each site has: Picnic table and fire ring

Site assignment: By campground management

Registration: By reservation up to 90 days in advance or on arrival

Facilities: Camp store, pay telephone, laundry room, and drink machine

Parking: Two vehicles per campsite

Fee: $15 per night

Elevation: Sea level

Restrictions:

Pets—On leash, not allowed in buildings, and not to be left unattended. Droppings must be picked up

Fires—Restricted to cooking pits; may not be left unattended; trash or any materials that carry sparks not to be used

Alcoholic beverages—Prohibited in public areas

Vehicles—No limit

Other—Loud noise is prohibited, quiet time 10 p.m. to 7 a.m.; no firearms or other weapons; swimming is prohibited; use water outlets for campsite only, no washing vehicles, dishes, clothes, or people; no more than 14 consecutive nights

NEWPORT NEWS PARK

Newport News

As development in the Hampton Roads area of Virginia increases with a similar expansion of traffic congestion, the 8,000-acre Newport News Park, one of the largest municipal parks east of the Mississippi River, shines brighter and brighter. Like many urban parks, Newport News Park offers a vast array of activities for both campers and day users, including a lake for boating and fishing, 18-hole golf course, five-star archery range, 30 miles of hiking trails, a family-oriented 5.3-mile bike path, and a 5-mile single-track mountain bike trail.

Newport News Park is located between downtown Newport News and Williamsburg along Interstate 64, Jefferson Avenue, and Fort Eustis Boulevard. After pulling off Jefferson Avenue into the park you'll need to stop at the camp store and office to register. Continuing along the park road, you'll see the six campground loops A–F on the right. The 180 campsites are nestled in the woods where both locals and travelers can pitch a tent and sleep under the stars while thousands of cars whiz by within earshot on I-64 and Jefferson Avenue.

Tent campers looking to leave the crowds behind will head for loop E which has the fewest hookups. At present, sites 123–132/144–157 on E loop have no hookups and will probably look the most attractive to minimalist campers. However, the park is adding hookups to all

CAMPGROUND RATINGS

Beauty:	★★★
Site privacy:	★★★
Site spaciousness:	★★★
Quiet:	★★★
Security:	★★
Cleanliness/upkeep:	★★★

Both locals and travelers can pitch a tent and sleep under the stars while thousands of cars whiz by within earshot on I-64 and Jefferson Avenue.

COASTAL

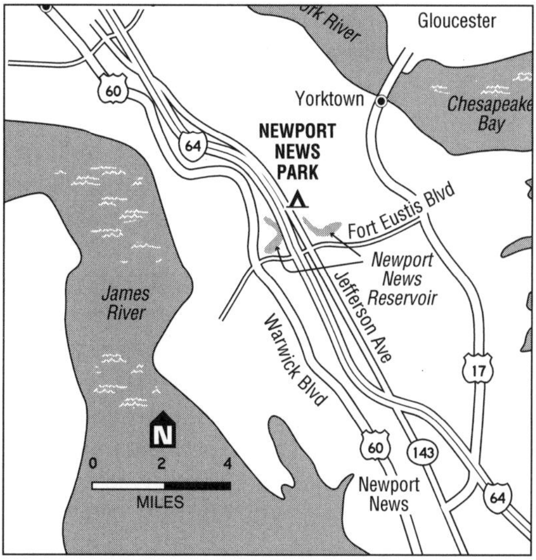

sites, so this information may quickly become moot. If you'd like to camp along the reservoir's edge, make a beeline for one of the following: B35-38, B41, 42, 44, 46, 48, 50, 51, and 53. Sites F171, 172, 174, 175, 177, and 178 are also waterfront. All sites are flat, offer ample separation from other sites, and lie within a grove of mature hardwoods with some understory. As is the case in any low-lying camping area, be sure to bring an ample supply of bug spray.

Some of you may camp here on the banks of Lee Hall Reservoir as an inexpensive alternative to local hotels and motels while still having access to the wealth of tourist attractions in Virgina's Peninsula region. However, the park itself offers quite a few recreational options within walking and biking distance. These include the archery range, two 18-hole golf courses, an 18-hole disc golf course, and a 30-acre aeromodel flying field. Nature programs that are suitable for children and adults are regularly scheduled in addition to the Children's Festival of Friends, the Newport News Fall Festival, and the Celebration in lights at Christmas when 450,000 lights transform the park into a magical world.

The park's bike path is popular among cyclists and joggers alike. It's flat, sandy surface offers the opportunity for some leisurely exercise for those of varied physical abilities. Those looking to expand their adventure past the park's boundaries can take the turn for Washington's Headquarters located between the two and three mile markers. Taking this detour provides access to the Colonial National Historical Park at Yorktown where the last battle of the Revolutionary War was fought in 1781.

Hikers can stretch their legs on 30 additional miles of trails that join the bike trail but are restricted to those who are hoofing it. Especially interesting to nature lovers will be the trails located in the park's swampy area between the Deer Run Golf Course and the Bike Path just off the eastern edge of the Lee Hall Reservoir.

Jon boats, canoes, and paddleboats are likewise available for rent should you want to fish for bass, pickerel, pike, or perch or just want to take a leisurely ride around the 650 acres of freshwater provided by the park's two reservoirs.

Be sure to stop by the Interpretive Center to get a better idea of the park's place in the past and present. With some three dozen species of mammals, over 200 species of birds, Civil War earthworks, and a number of family events, the amount of activities is considerable especially should you decide to drive a few miles. Those trying to stay in touch with Mother Nature will want to visit the nearby Virginia Living Museum with its live animal exhibits in natural habitat, planatarium, and 4,000-gallon ocean acquarium. For the rest of you, Colonial Williamsburg, Busch Gardens, and Water Country USA are all within a half-hour's drive of your camp site. You can pick up additional information about area attractions from the park headquarters and Tourist Information Center just east of the entrance for the campsite office on Jefferson Avenue.

To get there: From I-64, take exit 250B and follow the signs a short distance on Jefferson Avenue.

KEY INFORMATION

Newport News Park
13564 Jefferson Avenue
Newport News, VA 23603

Operated by: City of Newport Parks Department

Information: (757) 886-7912

Open: Year-round

Individual sites: 180

Each site has: Picnic table, fire ring, and grill

Site assignment: Campers can choose from available sites

Registration: By phone, (800) 203-8322; or on arrival

Facilities: Laundry room, camp store, hot showers, water, flush toilets, pay phones, and drink machine

Parking: Two private vehicles per campsite

Fee: $14 per night/$16.50 with electricity

Elevation: 40 feet

Restrictions:

Pets—On leash only with proof of rabies vaccination

Fires—Must be attended; dead and down wood may be collected for firewood

Other—Tents must be pitched within 25 feet of the pad with no more than two tents per site and only one camping vehicle per site; quiet hours 11 p.m. to 8 a.m.; length of stay 21 days within a 30-day period from April 1 through October 31

KIPTOPEKE STATE PARK

Cape Charles

CAMPGROUND RATINGS

Beauty: ★★★★
Site privacy: ★★★
Site spaciousness: ★★★
Quiet: ★★★★
Security: ★★★
Cleanliness/upkeep: ★★★★

The drive across and under the bay and the $10 one-way toll is a small price to pay for the tranquility that you'll find on the Eastern Shore.

Kiptopeke State Park is located at the southern end of Virginia's Eastern Shore just 3 miles from the 20-mile Chesapeake Bay Bridge-Tunnel. Separated from the "mainland" of the Old Dominion by the bridge-tunnel, the Eastern Shore is an entirely different world with a much slower pace than you left behind in Norfolk. The drive across and under the bay and the $10 one-way toll is a small price to pay for the tranquility that you'll find on the Eastern Shore. This 375-acre park offers 4,276 feet of beach frontage for swimming, surf casting, or just a leisurely stroll while watching the sunset.

After leaving US 13 and entering Kiptopeke (which translates to big water), you'll find the campground on the right just a short distance up the park's main road. The campsites are arranged in rows and vary from full hookups to no hookups and from open field to dense pine woods. The campsites get more wooded with higher numbers: 1–94 are mostly open and 95–141 are wooded (and offer minimal amenities). As you'd expect, the campground is very flat, so there are options as to how and where to set up your tent within any given site. In choosing your temporary homesite at Kiptopeke, however, keep in mind that woods can be both a plus and a minus when you're camping on the coast. While providing a modicum of privacy from other campers, the heavy

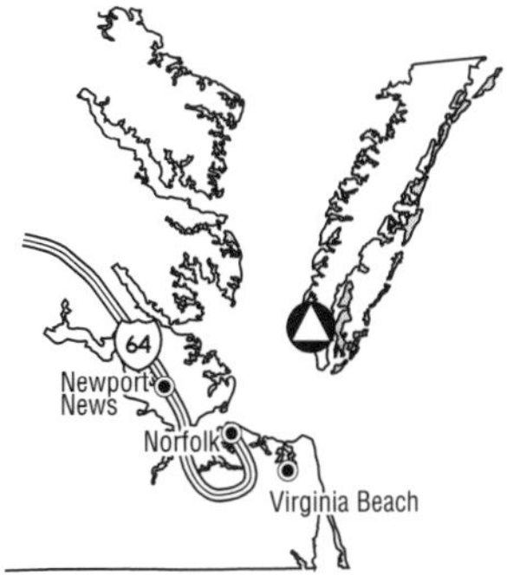

COASTAL

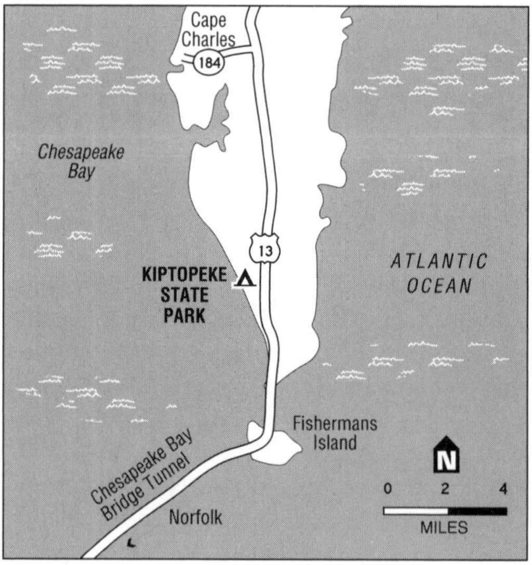

growth of pines and underbrush also cut off welcome breezes that can cool a sultry summer day and push pesky, six-legged critters right past your site. Boardwalks from the campground cross the sand dunes to reach the beach a short walk away.

Standing on the beach looking west across the Chesapeake, you're bound to wonder about those stationary ships just offshore. These nine concrete ships, sometimes called the Kiptopeke Navy, were purchased in 1948 to provide a harbor for the Virginia Ferry Corporation, which ran as many as 90 daily Chesapeake Bay crossings to Virginia Beach between 1933 and 1964 when the Chesapeake Bay Bridge-Tunnel was opened. Today these ships provide excellent habitat for saltwater trout, rockfish, striped bass, and flounder. A Virginia saltwater fishing license is required to fish from the shore, but none is needed when casting off the park's pier. The park also has its own boat launch with 4½ feet depth at mean low water.

Bird watchers flock to the area in October for the Eastern Shore Birding Festival and to observe some of the more than 200,000 birds of prey and migratory birds that use this flyway. The park has been the site of bird banding programs for population studies since 1963. Volunteers catch, examine, band, and release birds from September through November. The hawk observatory platform and banding station are located on the opposite side of the park road from the campground.

Additional birding grounds can be found at the Eastern Shore of Virginia National Wildlife Refuge located a short distance south on VA 13. To fully experience the refuge, be sure to check into taking a sea kayak tour offered by Southeast Expeditions (phone (877) KAYAK-11) in nearby Cheriton. If you're in search of a camping experience on the coast and want to leave the crowds behind, look no farther than Kiptopeke State Park.

To get there: From Norfolk, cross the Chesapeake Bay Bridge Tunnel on US 13. After three miles turn left onto VA 704 until you reach the park entrance.

KEY INFORMATION

Kiptopeke State Park
3540 Kiptopeke Drive
Cape Charles, VA 23310

Operated by: Virginia Department of Conservation and Recreation

Information: (757) 331-2267

Open: First weekend in March–December 1

Individual sites: 141

Each site has: Picnic table, fire ring, and lantern pole

Site assignment: Campers can choose from available sites

Registration: By phone, (800) 933-PARK; or at campground on arrival

Facilities: Hot showers, water, pay phone, and camp store

Parking: One motor vehicle in addition to camping unit per site

Fee: $18–$26 per night, depending on hookups

Elevation: Sea level

Restrictions:

Pets—On leash or in enclosed area and not allowed in swimming areas, on beach, or in toilet facilities

Fires—In fire rings, stoves, or grills only

Alcoholic beverages—Public use or display is prohibited

Vehicles—Up to 40 feet

Other—Do not carve, chop, or damage any live trees; hiking trails are for foot travel only; maximum of six people or one family per site; length of stay no more than 14 days in a 30-day period

CHIPPOKES PLANTATION STATE PARK

Surry

Located just across the James River from Jamestown, site of the first European settlement in the New World, Chippokes Plantation State Park dates from 1619 and is one of the oldest continuously farmed properties in the United States. The park's Farm and Forestry Museum displays thousands of artifacts, including a bull tongue plow which dates from the early 1600s. Exhibits show the various stages of farm life, such as preparing the soil, planting, cultivating, and harvesting as well as the related tasks of the blacksmith, wheelwright, cooper, and cobbler. The underlying theme is the succession of continual improvements in tools that were made to improve the lot of the farm family. Tours are also given through the 19th-century mansion on weekends from April through October. The formal gardens with their azaleas, crepe myrtle, and boxwood are a must-see. This side of the James is most directly accessible via the Jamestown-Scotland Wharf Ferry, with the closest bridges to the east in Newport News and to the west in Charles City County.

Shortly after turning into the park's main entrance, you'll see a sign for the campground on the right just across the park road from the swimming pool. The 32-site campground at this 1,683-acre setting is a relatively new addition to Chippokes, named for a Native American chief who befriended early English set-

CAMPGROUND RATINGS

Beauty:	★★★★
Site privacy:	★★★
Site spaciousness:	★★★
Quiet:	★★★
Security:	★★
Cleanliness/upkeep:	★★★★★

The summer of 1998 was the first full season that the campground was open, so campers may be pleasantly surprised to find empty sites until the word gets out about this hidden oasis.

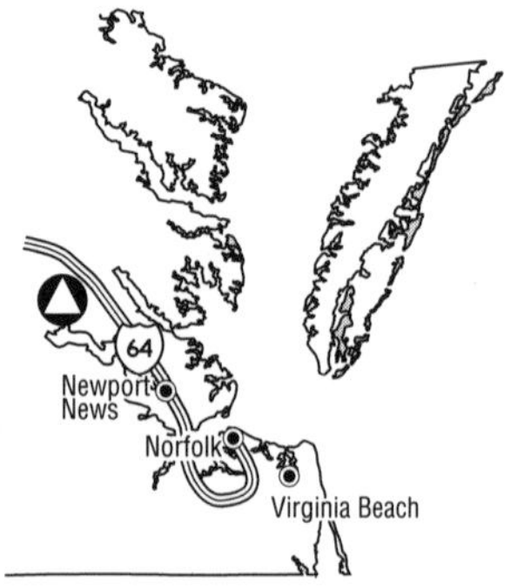

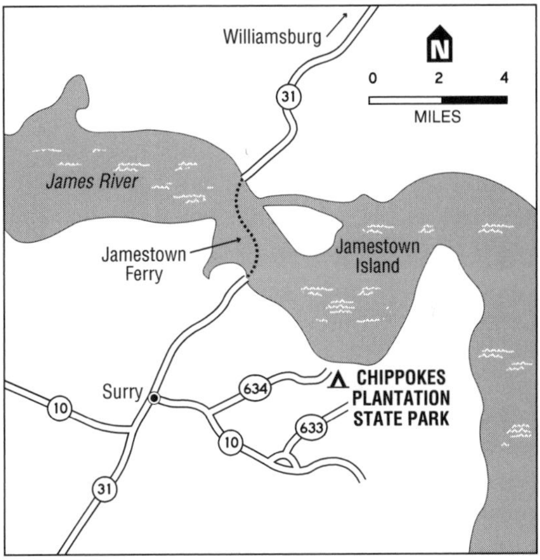

tlers. The summer of 1998 was the first full season that the campground was open, so campers may be pleasantly surprised to find empty sites until the word gets out about this hidden oasis. Hardwoods and pine surround the single campground loop, but none of the sites are especially secluded. This, however, can be a real bonus in a potentially buggy and humid area where even slight summer breezes are welcome. If privacy is an important criterion in site selection for you, take a look at sites 8, 12, 14, 17, 19, 23–26, and 32.

The park has 3.5 miles of paved trails for hikers and bikers. Scheduled nature activities include guided fossil hunts along the James River waterfront and canoe trips on the quiet streams that teem with both indigenous and migratory wildlife of the lower James River.

If you're looking to venture a little farther afield and continue your colonial history lessons, head over to Scotland Wharf (about five miles away) and from there take the 20-minute ferry ride to Jamestown. Colonial Williamsburg is a scant ten miles away on the Colonial Parkway, arguably one of the most beautiful roads in America. Another 15 miles on the parkway will take you to the Yorktown Battlefield, where the Revolutionary War ended. Those less interested in history and more intent on contemporary entertainment can head for Busch Gardens and Water Country USA from the north side of the James River.

Chippokes and I go back to the early 1970s when, as an undergraduate at the College of William and Mary, I would venture across the James River and pedal around the quiet, rural back roads of Surry County. Surry seems to have changed very little in the intervening twenty-some years, so road cycling along the county's little-traveled roads is still an enjoyable activity while visiting Chippokes.

An especially fun time to visit is in July when the annual Pork, Pine, and Peanut Festival is taking place at Chippokes, where you can sample some of the best pork and peanut dishes; enjoy down-home bluegrass, country, and gospel music; and admire the craftsmanship of over 200 artisans. Plans are presently underway to vastly expand the park's present facilities with a proposed $26 million educational Heritage Center. If all goes as planned, the expansion will be in place for the 400th anniversary of the settlement of Jamestown in 2007.

Park Manager Danette McAdoo suggests that campers should plan to spend at least a few days at Chippokes to get a complete picture of the natural and historic aspects of the park and surrounding Surry County. Birders, history buffs, and those who enjoy outdoor recreation will find a haven on the quiet side of the James River. Just be sure to bring ample insect repellent and an adventurous soul.

To get there: From Williamsburg, follow Jamestown Road/US 31 south until you reach the ferry dock at the James River. After crossing the river, continue south on US 31 into the town of Surry. Turn left at the center of town onto US 10 and then turn left onto VA 634. Continue for 4 miles until you reach the park entrance.

KEY INFORMATION

Chippokes Plantation State Park
695 Chippokes Park Road
Surry, VA 23883

Operated by: Virginia Department of Conservation and Recreation

Information: (757) 294-3625

Open: First weekend in March–December 1

Individual sites: 32

Each site has: Electricity, water, picnic table, lantern pole, fire ring, and tent pad

Site assignment: Campers can choose from available sites

Registration: By phone, (800) 933-PARK; or on arrival

Facilities: Hot showers, drink machines, and pay phone

Parking: One vehicle in addition to camping unit at campsite with additional parking at swimming pool

Fee: $22 per night

Elevation: 100 feet

Restrictions:

Pets—On leash or in enclosed area and not allowed in swimming areas or toilet facilities; $3 surcharge

Fires—In fire rings, stoves, or grills only

Alcoholic beverages—Prohibited

Vehicles—Up to 40 feet

Other—Do not carve, chop, or damage any live trees; keep noise at a reasonable level; no boat launching at park; length of stay no more than 14 days in a 30-day period

WESTMORELAND STATE PARK

Montross

Much has been written of the lofty Horsehead Cliffs linking Westmoreland State Park to the Potomac River, but on a recent visit to this coastal area during the yuletide season, it was not these platforms of turf-covered sand that commandeered our attention. As Dana and I strolled leisurely along sandy footpaths throughout the 1,299-acre park, it was the preponderance of holly, *Ilex opaca*, that stood out from the somber deciduous oak, hickory, and beech forest. Festooned with bright red berries set against shining green leaves, the holly branches sang of the season and filled the woods with cheer.

As pleasant as we found the off-season exploration of this park, one of Virginia's first six established in 1936, you'll undoubtedly want to explore Westmoreland between April and the end of November when its three campgrounds are open. After turning off US 3 in the village of Baynesville onto VA 347, you'll drive for a mile before reaching the park's contact station. Continuing on, you'll arrive first at campground C, on the right, where the park road's two lanes divide around a wooded medial strip. The first of these 40 sites alternate on either side of the campground road until a loop forms housing sites 14–40. It's on this loop that campers desiring a little privacy will want to pitch their nylon getaway. Site 34, in particular, is well secluded from the beaten path while

CAMPGROUND RATINGS

Beauty: ★★★★
Site privacy: ★★★
Site spaciousness: ★★★
Quiet: ★★★
Security: ★★★
Cleanliness/upkeep: ★★★★

You'll undoubtedly want to explore Westmoreland between April and the end of November when its three campgrounds are open.

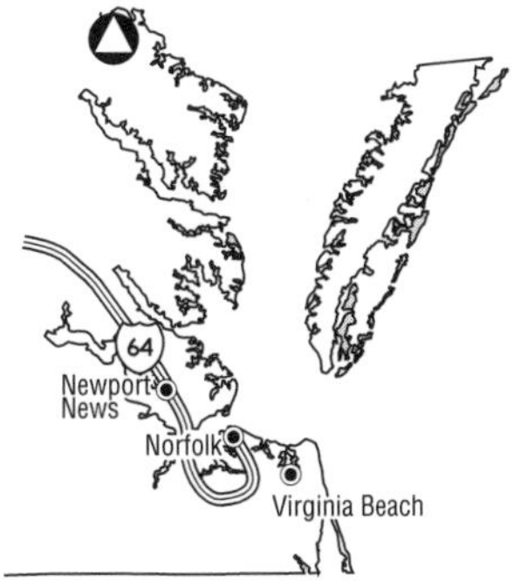

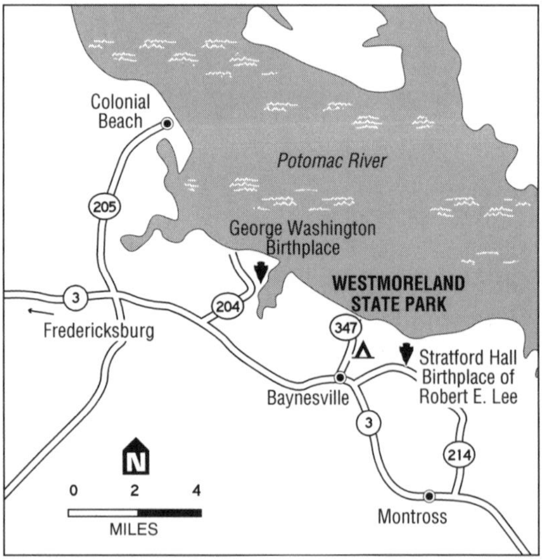

adjacent to the 2.5-mile Turkey Neck Trail, which loops around the eastern section of the park.

The dual lanes of the two-mile park road rejoin after a short distance, and you'll see campground B on the right. Just before the entrance is the trailhead for the 1.4-mile Laurel Point Trail, which loops around to the beachfront on the Potomac River. Fifty-six sites are well spread out within campground B along interconnected looping campground roads while thick plantings of holly provide a colorful understory beneath mature hardwoods. Approximately one-third of the sites offer electric and water hookups, but these sites are more conducive to pop-up campers than more imposing recreational vehicles. Especially enticing are sites 33–45 and 46–56, which are situated along their own smaller loops. Just after passing the park's visitor center and before The Park Restaurant, you'll notice campground A on the right side of the park road. These 43 sites are laid out on two loops to accommodate large RVs as well as the small cabins located here.

Westmoreland's main road curves past the rental cabin area before ending at Potomac River beachfront, where you'll find the park's boat landing and swimming pool. Anglers can fish for striped bass, spot, and bluefish from the pier or shore without a license, while fishing from a boat into the Potomac requires a Virginia or Maryland saltwater license. Six hiking trails wind through the park with the aforementioned Turkey Neck and Laurel Point being the longest. The others are all less than a mile and connect to the Turkey Neck and Laurel Point Trails. None of the trails are open to equestrians or bicyclists.

In addition to fishing, boating, and hiking on the park's maze of easy trails, you'll find a variety of outdoor activities including the old-fashioned Market Day, an orienteering meet sponsored by the Quantico Orienteering Club, and an outdoor photography workshop. And what better way to see the famed 140-foot Horsehead Cliffs up close than by taking one of the Kayak Below the Cliffs outings. Kids of all ages will enjoy hunting for sharks' teeth dating from some 23 million years ago at the base of the cliffs. History of a more recent nature abounds as well with the birthplaces of George Washington and Robert E. Lee just minutes away from Westmoreland State Park.

To get there: From I-95, take US 3 at Fredericksburg and drive for 40 miles to the town of Baynesville. Turn left onto VA 347 to enter the park.

KEY INFORMATION

Westmoreland State Park
Route 1, Box 600
Montross, VA 22520

Operated by: Virginia Department of Conservation and Recreation

Information: (804) 493-8821

Open: First weekend in March–December 1

Individual sites: 138

Each site has: Picnic table and fire grill

Site assignment: First come, first served

Registration: (800) 933-PARK in advance or on arrival

Facilities: Restaurant and camp store

Parking: At campsites, trailheads, and day-use area

Fee: $14/$18 per night with water and electricity

Elevation: 160 feet

Restrictions:

Pets—Must be kept in an enclosed area or on a leash shorter than six feet long

Fires—Must be confined to camp stoves and fire rings

Alcoholic beverages—Public use or display is prohibited

Vehicles—Up to 30 feet

Other—Swimming not allowed from shoreline due to motorboat traffic and underwater objects; length of stay no more than 14 days in a 30-day period

PIEDMONT CAMPGROUNDS

POCAHONTAS STATE PARK

Chesterfield

Whether you learned about Pocahontas through history class, legend, or the Disney animated movie, the name of this daughter of Chief Powhatan should be familiar to most. However, there is no connection between the Indian maiden who saved the life of John Smith and later married John Rolfe, and the park. It just happened to be the winning name suggested by a third-grader in a park-naming contest after the Civilian Conservation Corps built the park in the 1930s. The National Park Service operated what was originally known as the Swift Creek Recreation Area until 1946 when it was donated to the Commonwealth of Virginia.

Pocahontas State Park's 7,600 acres make it the largest park in the Virginia state park system, an especially impressive fact given that it lies a mere 20 miles from the state capital of Richmond. Indeed, a large appeal of this vast green space is its accessibility for both travelers and residents to a major urban and suburban area. As a graduate student at nearby Virginia Commonwealth University and a live-in camp director residing several miles down the road, I spent a good bit of time at Pocahontas State Park in the late 1970s.

Much has changed at this Chesterfield County location over the years, including a recent major campground reconstruction project. The original 34-site campground constructed by the CCC on a hillside along

CAMPGROUND RATINGS

Beauty: ★★★★
Site privacy: ★★★
Site spaciousness: ★★★
Quiet: ★★★
Security: ★★★
Cleanliness/upkeep: ★★★★

Despite the park's suburban location and considerable day use, its size and preponderance of mature hardwoods help it maintain a feeling of sanctuary.

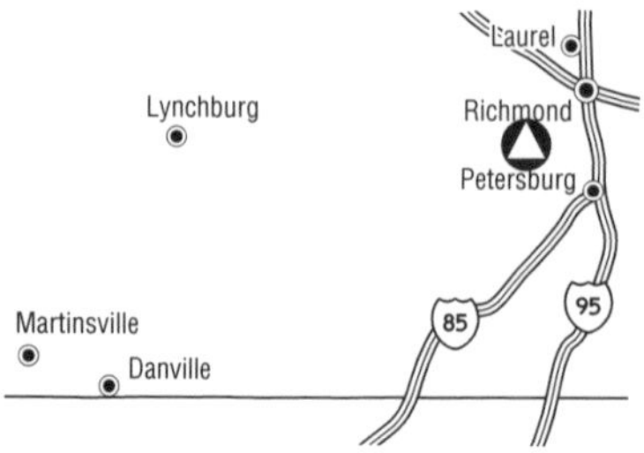

PIEDMONT

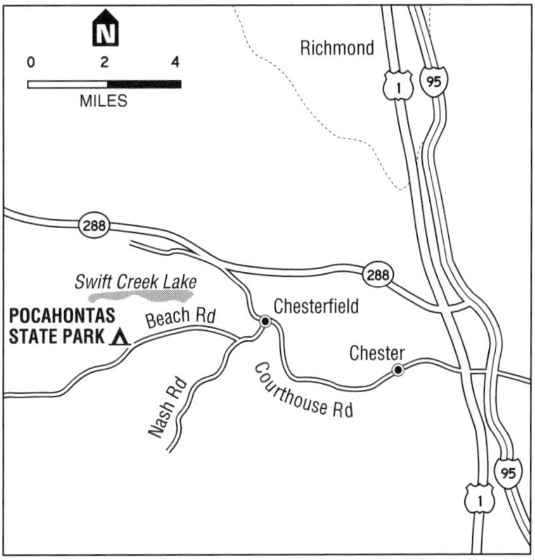

Swift Creek has given way to a larger facility with full electric and water hookups. While the quaintness of the former setting may have been lost to us tent campers with the new, more RV-friendly campground, there are numerous sites that offer a modicum of privacy and solitude.

After turning off Beach Road at the park's entrance, you'll drive down the wide forest-lined park road for a mile before reaching the contact station, after which you'll see the campground entrance on the right. The 65 campsites are situated along the main access road and loops A, B, and C against a dense backdrop of mature oaks with shorter holly and pine trees.

Despite the park's suburban location and considerable day use by Richmonders, its size and preponderance of mature hardwoods help it maintain a feeling of sanctuary. However, during the summer when things are really hopping at Pocahontas, you may find yourself bumping elbows with other campers and day users alike.

Hikers and mountain bikers can enjoy more than 25 miles of forest roads and trails that meander throughout the park. Some trails circle the 24-acre Beaver Lake, while others wend their way through the hardwood forest. Those out for a leisurely stroll will enjoy the 2.5-mile Beaver Lake Trail, and the 3.2-mile Old Mill Bicycle Trail offers an easy pedal through the park. Fat-tire bicyclists looking for a greater challenge will head for the three newly constructed technical single-track trails that were built as a joint effort between Pocahontas State Park and Mountain Bike Virginia (the club, not my previously published book of the same name). Be sure to pick up copies of the Pocahontas Park Guide and Bike Trails Guide. There are also nine miles of bridal paths for equestrian use on a BYOH (Bring Your Own Horse) basis.

Whether you plan to hide out in the "wilds" of Chesterfield County or use Pocahontas State Park as a base camp from which to explore the city of Richmond, you're guaranteed to find this an inviting destination.

To get there: From I-95 take Exit 61 and go west on VA 10 past the village of Chester. Turn left onto Beach Road at the traffic light across from the old Chesterfield County Courthouse complex. Go 5 miles and turn right into the park's entrance.

KEY INFORMATION

Pocahontas State Park
10301 State Park Road
Chesterfield, VA 23838-4713

Operated by: Virginia Department of Conservation and Recreation

Information: (804) 796-4255

Open: First weekend in March–December 1

Individual sites: 65

Each site has: Picnic table, lantern pole, fire ring, and electric/water hookups

Site assignment: First come, first served

Registration: (800) 933-PARK

Facilities: Bathhouses with hot showers and flush toilets, pay telephones, and drink machines

Parking: One camping unit and the camping unit per site. Additional parking adjacent to contact station.

Fee: $18 per night

Elevation: 200 feet

Restrictions:

Pets—$3 extra per night, must be kept on leash or in enclosed area

Fires—Confined to grills, camp stoves, or designated fire rings

Alcoholic beverages—Prohibited

Vehicles—Up to 30 feet

Other—Do not carve, chop, or damage any live trees; no motorized vehicles on state park trails; swimming only in designated area during operating hours; no gasoline motors on lake; length of stay no more than 14 days in a 30-day period

BEAR CREEK LAKE STATE PARK

Cumberland

CAMPGROUND RATINGS

Beauty: ★★★★
Site privacy: ★★
Site spaciousness: ★★★
Quiet: ★★
Security: ★★★
Cleanliness/upkeep: ★★★★

Visitors to Bear Creek Lake State Park can choose from an array of outdoor activities, including the Virginia park system's only archery range.

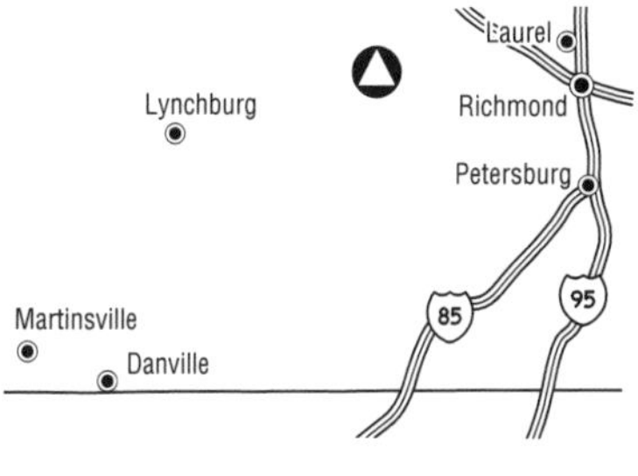

Bear Creek Lake State Park is located in Central Virginia's piedmont region, nestled in the shade of mature towering sweet gum, oak, and tulip polar trees. The park has three small campgrounds designated A, B, and C. Campground A is just behind the camp office and sits on a hillside overlooking the lake. The campground host's site is adjacent to the park road at site A-25. The sites are fairly close together, although each has more than adequate size for a tent and other camping gear. However, given a choice, try to snag site 10, 11, or 17, all of which hug the lake. The small loop encompassing sites A5–A13 has no hookups and will appeal to self-sufficient tent campers.

Campground B, located across the road from the camp office, offers electric and water hookups and appeared to be the busiest of the three. Its single loop provides 20 sites that are fairly close together under a roof of mature hardwoods, but it lacks a bathhouse.

Campground C is a little farther up on the left side of the camp road. The sites lack hookups, but the single loop is flat and has its own bathhouse. This loop contains ten sites with 8 and 10 seemingly the most private. The quarter-mile Running Cedar Trail is just across the road and provides access to the Lakeside Trail and swimming beach.

Visitors to Bear Creek Lake State Park can choose from an array of outdoor activities,

PIEDMONT

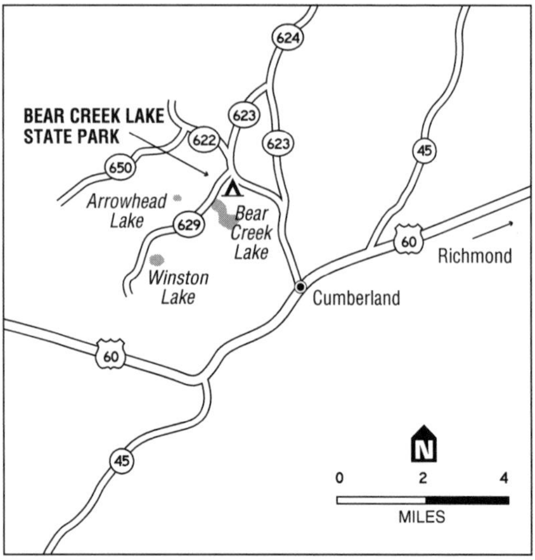

including the Virginia park system's only archery range. Ten bale targets with assorted big game faces are set against natural backdrops to simulate the hunting experience with varied shooting stations designated by color to allow consistent scoring. The range is open year-round, although closing time on any given day is dictated by light conditions and safety.

The swimming area and sand beach on this 40-acre lake are refreshing spots during the heat of the summer, but anglers can fish throughout the year for largemouth bass, crappie, bream, and channel catfish. Canoeists can enjoy a lazy paddle around the lake or a bit more spirited run down the Willis River, which winds through the Cumberland State Forest. Various styles of aquacraft are available for rent during the summer. Or check out one of the in-season family canoe tours. There are a number of other area lakes, including Winston Lake, Arrowhead Lake, Oakhill Lake, and Bonbrook Lake, all of which provide ample fishing opportunities. A Virginia fishing license is required for those 16 years of age and older.

There are a number of trails, both within the 326-acre park and in the surrounding 16,233-acre Cumberland State Forest. The 1.5-mile (point-to-point) orange-blazed Lakeside Trail and 3-mile white-blazed Circumferential loop trail hug opposite sides of the lake. The Lakeside Trail stretches from Campground A past the lakeside picnic area and beach before connecting with the Pine Knob and Circumferential Trail. Shorter walks in the park include the blue-blazed Running Cedar Trail, the 0.4-mile yellow-blazed Quail Ridge Trail, and quarter-mile gray-blazed Pine Knob Trail.

Hikers, equestrians, and mountain bikers looking for a longer jaunt can choose from either the blue-blazed 14-mile Cumberland Multi-Use loop trail or the 16-mile (point-to-point) Willis River Trail. The relatively new multi-use trail is fairly flat with the exception of sections that traverse riparian areas and wind throughout Cumberland State Forest on forest roads, state roads, and single track. Parking is located next to the archery range. Although a linear rather than a loop trail, all points of the Willis River Trail are within ten miles of Bear Creek Lake State Park and can be accessed from numerous intersections with county and state forest roads. Also located near the park in Cumberland State Forest is a ten-station sporting clay range.

To get there: From US 60, drive 4.5 miles northwest of the town of Cumberland. Go west on VA 622 and then south on VA 629 to the park entrance.

KEY INFORMATION

Bear Creek Lake State Park
Route 1, Box 253
Cumberland, VA 23040

Operated by: Virginia Department of Conservation and Recreation

Information: (804) 492-4410

Open: First weekend in March–December 1

Individual sites: 53

Each site has: Picnic table, grill

Site assignment: Choose from available sites

Registration: By phone, (800) 933-PARK; or at campground on arrival

Facilities: Laundry sinks, pay phone, and hot showers

Parking: One vehicle in addition to camping unit allowed at site, additional parking at office

Fee: $11; $15 per night with electric and water hookups

Elevation: 270 feet

Restrictions:

Pets—$3 extra per night; must be kept on leash or in enclosed area

Fires—Confined to grills, camp stoves, or designated fire rings

Alcoholic beverages—Prohibited

Vehicles—Up to 30 feet

Other—Do not carve, chop, or damage any live trees; no motorized vehicles on state park trails; swimming only in designated area during operating hours; no gasoline motors on lake; length of stay no more than 14 days in a 30-day period

FAIRY STONE STATE PARK

Stuart

Legend has it that a long time ago, fairies inhabited the foothills of the Blue Ridge Mountains in this section of Virginia near the North Carolina border. One day their play was interrupted by an elfin messenger who'd come from a distant city to bring news about the death of Christ. Their grief was tremendous, and as their tears touched the earth, they formed beautiful crosses that symbolized the crucifixion. Although the fairies disappeared, these stone crosses remained and can still be found here today. Wearers of these fairy crosses long believed that they warded off witchcraft, sickness, accidents, and disaster. You may not put much stock in the myth, but there is no place in the world that offers either the quantity or quality of shape of these brown staurolite crosses as Fairy Stone State Park.

Locate the recommended spot for finding these unique stones by leaving the park and heading east on US 57 toward Bassett. After about 2.5 miles you'll notice an old gas station (Haynes Store) on the left. A sign identifies the park-owned property and streambed where the crosses can be collected for personal use. My 13-year-old, Chris, and I wandered along looking for these staurolite crosses with limited success. He half-expected the crystals to jump off the ground and into his hands, while I merely hoped that would be the case. The best time to go hunting is after a rain, but I was still able to find several examples during a dry

CAMPGROUND RATINGS

Beauty: ★★★
Site privacy: ★★
Site spaciousness: ★★
Quiet: ★★★
Security: ★★★
Cleanliness/upkeep: ★★★

The campground lies on one of the many hilltops here in the foothills of the Blue Ridge Mountains.

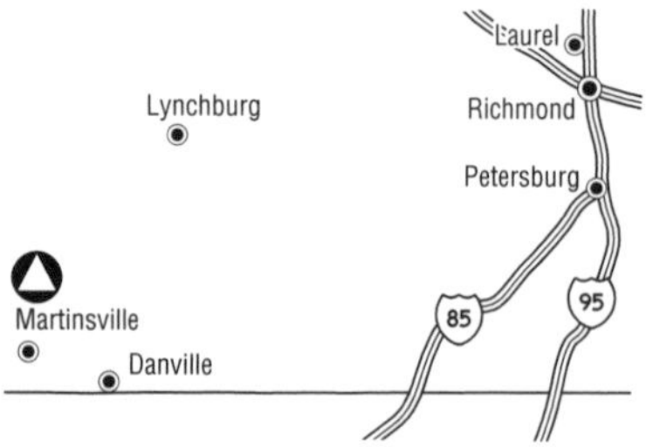

PIEDMONT

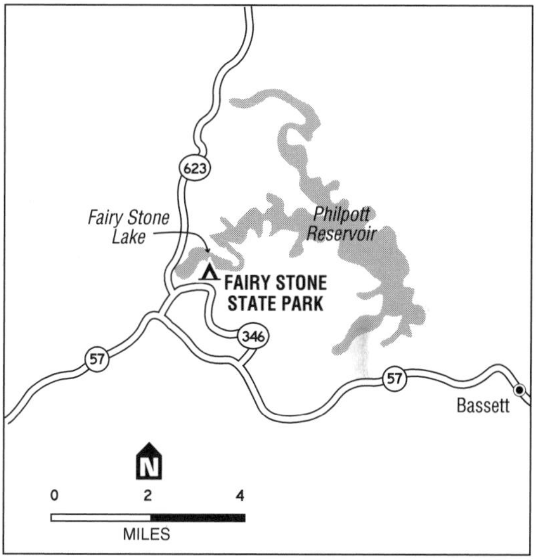

spell. You're more likely to find the crystals still embedded in bits of schist, which is more easily weathered away, so patience and a good eye are essential. The judicious use of a file will bring out one of several shapes in which they form. However, should you come up empty-handed, Haynes Store offers a good selection at reasonable prices.

Fairy Stone was one of the six original parks in Virginia's park system in 1936. Its 4,868 acres made it the largest then, and it is still one of the largest today. After passing the 168-acre Fairy Stone Lake and beachfront on the left, you'll arrive at the contact station and the park office to the left of it. Straight ahead is the visitor center, where you'll want to stop to see the extensive collection of fairy stones as well as information about the local history and plant and animal life. Bear right at the visitor center and continue a short distance up the road until you reach the entrance to the campground on the left.

The campground lies on one of the many hilltops here in the foothills of the Blue Ridge Mountains. The 51 sites, all with electric and water hookups, enjoy the shade of a pine grove with some scattered oaks. The majority of the campsites have sand tent pads, with the exception of several pull-throughs. The single loop is located in the center of the park and well off local roads, with a dense barrier of pines and hardwoods surrounding the campground. There are also thick stands of wild rhododendron throughout the park; an especially large one is across from the picnic area leading up to the campground.

There are several hiking trails that range in length and degree of challenge from the 0.9-mile Beach Trail, which leads from site 28 to the lake and beach, to the orange-blazed Little Mountain Falls Trail. This 4.2-mile trail is accessible just across the road from the campground via the gated 2.1-mile Mountain View Hiking and Bicycle Trail. If you plan to do any hiking, be sure to pick up one of the park's *Stuart's Knob and Little Mountain Trail Systems Guides.*

To get there: From I-81 near Roanoke, take I-581 to US 220. Follow this to Bassett Forks and turn right onto US 57. Turn right onto VA 346 until you reach the park's entrance.

KEY INFORMATION

Fairy Stone State Park
967 Fairystone Lake Drive
Stuart, VA 24171

Operated by: Virginia Department of Conservation and Recreation

Information: (540) 930-2424

Open: First weekend in March–December 1

Individual sites: 51

Each site has: Picnic table, fire grill, and water/electric hookup

Site assignment: First come, first served

Registration: By phone, (800) 933-PARK; or at campground on arrival

Facilities: Flush toilets, hot showers, pay telephone, and drink machines (by the lakefront sandy beach)

Parking: One vehicle in addition to camping unit; additional parking a half-mile away

Fee: $15 per night; $18 on weekends

Elevation: 1,240 feet

Restrictions:

Pets—Must be on six-foot leash and attended; additional fee charged per night

Fires—Confined to camp stoves and fire rings

Alcoholic beverages—Prohibited

Vehicles—Up to 30 feet

Other—No cutting or marring of vegetation; length of stay no more than 14 days in a 30-day period

HOLLIDAY LAKE STATE PARK

Appomattox

Compulsive spellers, amateur editors, and nitpickers should take note that this park is named for the "Holliday" family farm whose remnants lie at the bottom of the lake, and any use of two L's is purely intentional. With that bit of concern aside, you can feel free to enjoy the facilities that the 250-acre Holliday Lake State Park has to offer. The campground is located to the right of the park road just after passing the contact station. It sits on the side of a hill; but fear not, the 30 sites are level and spacious, allowing ample space to pitch your tent. The backdrop of mature hardwoods offers a woodsy feel to the area, but the sites themselves are fairly open. Like most state parks, the summer is a busy time here at Holliday Lake State Park and reservations are highly recommended.

The park land and surrounding landscape were cleared for farming in the 1800s. However, the federal Resettlement Administration began buying local tracts to return it to hardwood forest. The lake itself was constructed under the Works Projects Administration and completed in 1938. All the work was done by hand with the assistance of mules and dynamite. The Commonwealth of Virginia took over managing, what was then a day-use recreational area, and Holliday Lake became a state park in 1972 with the addition of the campground.

CAMPGROUND RATINGS

Beauty: ★★★★
Site privacy: ★★
Site spaciousness: ★★★★
Quiet: ★★
Security: ★★★
Cleanliness/upkeep: ★★★★

The backdrop of mature hardwoods offers a woodsy feel to the area.

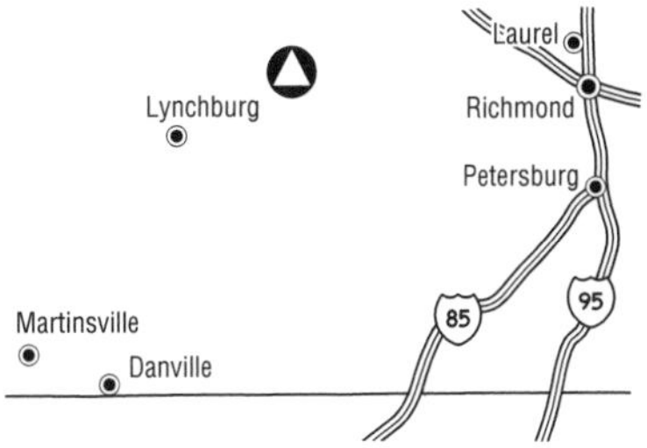

PIEDMONT

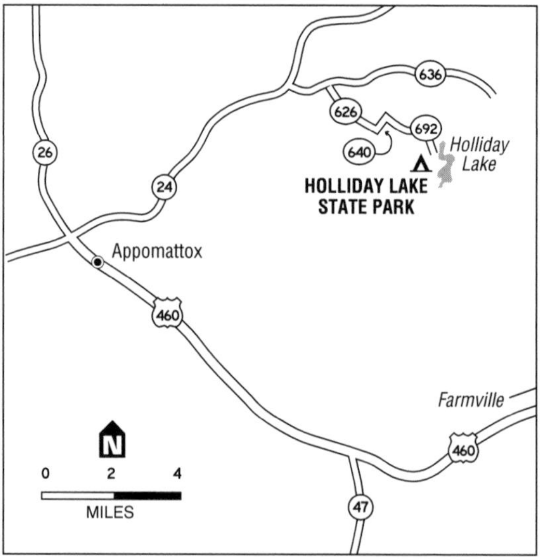

The short Saunders Creek Trail connects the campground and lakefront area. Here you'll find picnic shelters, a boat launch, and swimming beach. Whether you want to fish the 150-acre lake for bass, northern pike, crappie, sunfish, or channel catfish, you'll want to bring a boat (only electric motors can be used) or rent one to do some aquatic exploration. A Virginia fishing license is required to fish at Holliday Lake. The sandy beachfront swimming area offers a great way to cool off during the summer's heat or have a lunch alfresco in the shady, lakefront picnic area.

Besides swimming, fishing, and boating, another attraction here is the relatively new 12-mile Carter Taylor loop trail, which starts inside the park across from the campground. After quickly leaving the park and entering the surrounding 19,710-acre Appomattox-Buckingham State Forest, the CT Trail utilizes state forest and state roads as well as the occasional stretch of singletrack. Pick up a copy of the Carter Taylor Trail brochure, which shows the route of the multi-use trail open to hikers, bicyclists, and equestrians.

There are also shorter trails within the park's boundaries including the one-mile Dogwood Ridge Trail and the five-mile Lakeshore Nature Trail. The state forest is Virginia's largest with a considerable network of woods roads that are likewise open to hikers, bikers, and equestrians. Those venturing out into the state forest should get a forest service map to stay oriented on the Carter Taylor as well as for assistance in developing additional routes through the rolling countryside.

Civil War buffs will not want to miss the opportunity to visit the Appomattox Court House National Historic Park where Confederate General Robert E. Lee surrendered to Union General Ulysses S. Grant to end the Civil War, more commonly known here in Virginia as the War of Northern Aggression. Lee's Army of Northern Virginia, weary and tattered, passed approximately 1.5 miles from the present park site en route to the final battles of the war. The park encompasses some 1,700 acres of rolling hills with self-guided walking tours on the six-mile History Trail, audio visual programs, and various other interpretive programs presented by park personel. The park's visitor center is located in the reconstructed courthouse on US 24 just two miles northeast of the town of Appomattox.

To get there: From US 460, turn onto US 24 in the town of Appomattox. After 8 miles, turn right onto VA 626 and follow this for 3.4 miles. Turn left onto VA 640, and then right onto VA 692. Continue 2.5 miles to the park's entrance.

KEY INFORMATION

Holliday Lake State Park
Route 2, Box 622
Appomattox, VA 24522

Operated by: Virginia Department of Conservation and Recreation

Information: (804) 248-6308

Open: First weekend in March–December 1

Individual sites: 30

Each site has: Water, electricity, picnic table, fire grill, and lantern pole

Site assignment: Campers can choose from available sites

Registration: By phone, (800) 933-PARK; or at campground on arrival

Facilities: Camp store, flush toilets, and water

Parking: One vehicle in addition to camping unit allowed at site

Fee: $15 per night, $18 with hookups

Elevation: 470 feet

Restrictions:

Pets—Must be on six-foot leash and attended; additional fee charged

Fires—Confined to fireplaces, fire rings, and camp stoves

Alcoholic beverages—Public use or display is prohibited

Vehicles—No limit

Other—Maximum stay is 14 days in a 30-day period; sites are limited to six people or a single family

TWIN LAKES STATE PARK

Green Bay

Twin Lakes State Park is located near Farmville in a shady area of mature hardwoods and includes Goodwin Lake and Prince Edward Lake from which the 425-acre park got its name. Two racially segregated parks began operations in 1939 and continued in this fashion into the early 1960s. They merged in 1976 and became Twin Lakes State Park in 1986. The park's main road and the 0.25-mile Between the Lakes Trail connect the two units. Facilities at Goodwin Lake are available for individual camping, picnicking, and swimming; group camping, a lodge, and cabins at the Cedar Crest Conference Center sit on the eastern shore of Prince Edward Lake. The center is available by reservation only with cabin rentals possible when not booked already by groups.

After entering the park off of VA 629, you'll find the campground located opposite the contact station. It consists of a large loop with a smaller loop at the rear. All of the sites are spacious, include water and electric hookups, and are set off by a dense wooded background which provides ample shade during the summer. Site 11, located at the back of the smaller loop that encompasses sites 6–15, is the most private of all. Tent pads are gravel, so be sure to pack a ground cloth for your tent and sleeping pad.

The day-use area at Goodwin Lake includes the 1.5-mile Goodwin Lake Nature

CAMPGROUND RATINGS

Beauty: ★★★
Site privacy: ★★
Site spaciousness: ★★★
Quiet: ★★★
Security: ★★★
Cleanliness/upkeep: ★★★

The 6,970-acre Prince Edward-Gallion State Forest surrounds the park and offers an array of gated forest roads that are open to hikers and bikers.

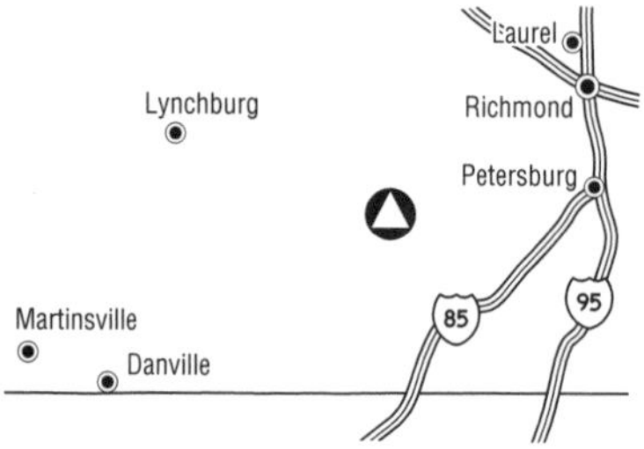

PIEDMONT

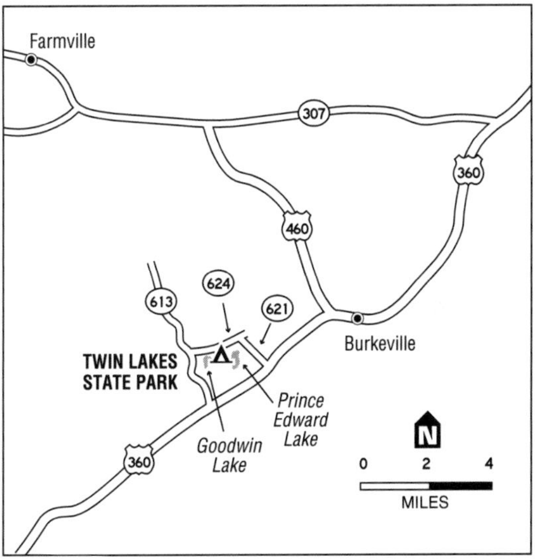

Trail, sandy beach, picnic tables, and a playground. Those looking for a longer hike can try the four-mile Otter's Path Nature Loop Trail. A relatively new addition is the 14-mile Multi-Use Trail, which winds around through the adjacent 6,496-acre Prince Edward-Gallion State Forest. This trail is open is hikers, bikers, and equestrians alike.

I revisited this park as well as nearby Bear Creek Lake State Park and Holliday Lake State Park on a warm, sunny Saturday in September, and was surprised to find Twin Lakes' campground to be almost empty while the other two were full. Swimming is allowed off the designated beachfront area of Goodwin Lake, and either lake can be used by boaters and fishermen.

There are several of hiking trails which range from the 0.25-mile yellow-blazed Between the Lakes Trail to the fairly strenuous, orange-blazed, 4-mile Otter's Path Nature Trail which circles Prince Edward Lake. Also popular is the 1.5-mile, blue-blazed Goodwin Lake Nature Trail, which is less taxing and provides a number of interpretive signs describing the area's flora and fauna as it circles the smaller of the two lakes.

The 6,970-acre Prince Edward-Gallion State Forest surrounds the park and offers an array of gated forest roads that are open to hikers and bikers. Pick up a map of the forest and plan an outing that will take you through areas of various stages of vegetative succession and home to racoons, muskrats, white-tailed deer, wild turkey, and quail.

Civil War buffs will want to visit nearby Sailor's Creek Historical State Park, site of the last major battle in the war. General Robert E. Lee's army lost 7,000 men on April 6, 1865, leading to his surrender at Appomattox Courthouse 72 hours later. A former federal field hospital is open to the public on a limited schedule; and re-enactments and encampments are but part of the "living history" at Sailor's Creek. It is part of Lee's Retreat Driving Tour, which leads from Petersburg to Appomattox, so you can tune to AM 1610 on your car radio to learn more about the preceding events and the battle itself that ended the Civil War.

To get there: From Richmond, drive for approximately 50 miles on US 360 through the town of Burkeville. Turn right onto VA 613 at the sign for Twin Lakes, and then turn right after a mile onto VA 629. Turn left into the campground entrance after driving 2 miles.

KEY INFORMATION

Twin Lakes State Park
Route 2, Box 70
Green Bay, VA 23942

Operated by: Virginia Department of Conservation and Recreation

Information: (804) 392-3435

Open: First weekend in March–December 1

Individual sites: 33

Each site has: Electricity, water, fire grill, and picnic table

Site assignment: Campers can choose from available sites

Registration: By phone, (800) 933-PARK; or at campground on arrival

Facilities: Bathhouse with hot showers and flush toilets, soda machine, pay telephone

Parking: One vehicle at campsite in addition to camping unit; additional parking at day-use area

Fee: $15 per night

Elevation: 450 feet

Restrictions:

Pets—$3 extra per night; must be kept on six-foot leash or in enclosed area

Fires—Confined to grills, camp stoves, or designated fire rings

Alcoholic beverages—Public use or display is prohibited

Vehicles—Up to 25 feet

Other—Do not carve, chop, or damage any live trees; no motorized vehicles on state park trails; swimming only in designated area during operating hours; length of stay no more than 14 days in a 30-day period

SMITH MOUNTAIN LAKE STATE PARK

Huddleston

CAMPGROUND RATINGS

Beauty:	★★★
Site privacy:	★★
Site spaciousness:	★★★
Quiet:	★★★
Security:	★★★★
Cleanliness/upkeep:	★★★

The park is spread out over 1,248 densely wooded acres of Virginia pine, American beech, and juniper.

As you might deduce from this park's name, Smith Mountain Lake is the central focus here. This 20,000-acre, 50-mile-long body of water is Virginia's second largest freshwater lake. Bass anglers come from far and wide to land the citation largemouth and stripers that are caught every year during recreational and tournament fishing. A Virginia freshwater license is required whether fishing from the shore, a boat, or the fishing pier at the boat launch. Appalachian Power Company created the lake in 1960 by damming the Roanoke River, and the park opened later in 1983. However, Smith Mountain Lake State Park is no less a great destination for tent campers looking for a little solitude in the foothills of the Blue Ridge Mountains. In fact, if you remained at the campground during your entire stay, you'd never see the lake, which is rather inconspicuous unless you ride down over to the visitor center, boat launch, or beachfront swimming area.

The 500-foot sandy beach is the park's only swimming area and features a bathhouse and concessionaire open during the summer. Paddleboats, jet skis, and pontoon boats are available for rent during this period. Other activities at Smith Mountain Lake State Park include guided night hikes, hayrides, canoe trips, and twilight programs, in addition to the Junior Rangers program for children six to ten years old.

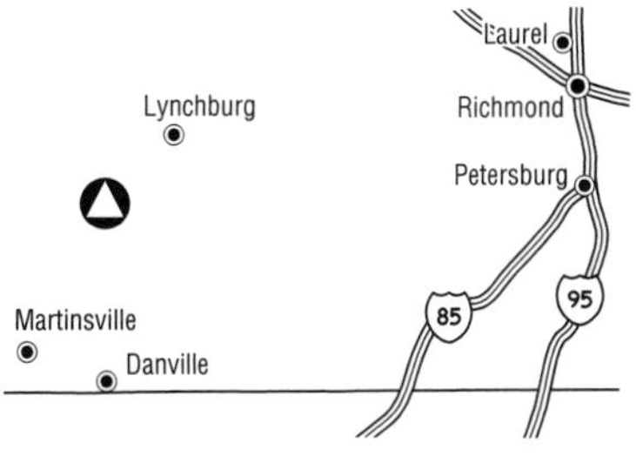

PIEDMONT

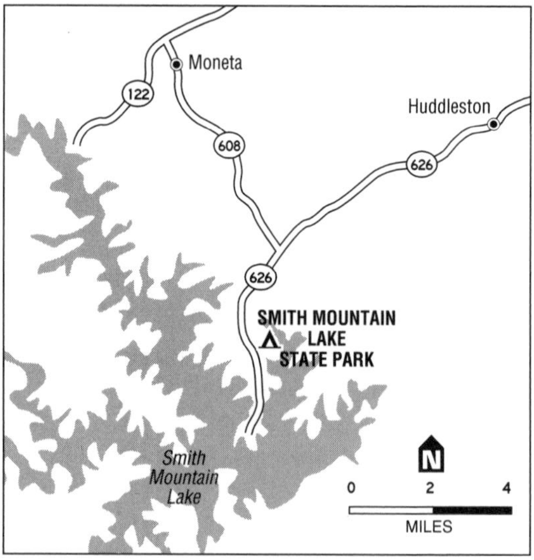

Another popular spot is the picnic area located adjacent to the swimming area. Be sure to stop by the park's visitor center, where you'll find interesting exhibits describing area history, folklore, and environment.

The park is spread out over 1,248 densely wooded acres of Virginia pine, American beech, and juniper, which provide a back-to-nature feel while keeping the lake out of sight. The campground, visitor center, and boat launch/swimming area are situated on three separate peninsulas, so access from one to the other is best handled by car. You can also reach the water by way of the trails, which range in length from the 0.8-mile Lake View Trail to the 1.5-mile Chestnut Ridge. Just outside the gated entrance to the visitor center is a kiosk and trailhead for the 1.3-mile Turtle Island Trail, and the 0.5-mile Beechwood Trail is accessible from the dump station located next to the campground entrance. All of these trails will provide an easy to moderate excursion for hikers of average physical condition.

After entering the park from VA 626, you'll see the park office on the right past the contact station. Turn left onto Interpretive Trail Road across from the office, and then turn left onto Overnight Road. You'll find the campground on the right with overflow parking across the road. The campground consists of dual loops on which 50 sites are located. Sites 16–26, 27–35, and 42–47 lack hookups and are set off a short distance in the woods. Access to these sites requires a short walk from your car, but the additional privacy is worth it.

The other sites are located along the campground loop and set fairly close together. Like the rest of the park, the campground is set among a mixture of conifers and deciduous trees offering plentiful shade. The presence of 20 rental cabins is a fairly new addition to Smith Mountain Lake and may ease the pressure on the very popular campground. With Smith Mountain Lake's popularity as a destination for bass fishermen, it's especially advisable to plan your arrival during the week in the summer for optimum solitude.

To get there: From Roanoke, head east on US 460 to Bedford. From there proceed south on VA 122 to Moneta. Go east on VA 608, and then head south for 2 miles on VA 626 to the park entrance.

KEY INFORMATION

Smith Mountain Lake State Park
1235 State Park Road
Huddleston, VA 24104-9547

Operated by: Virginia Department of Conservation and Recreation

Information: (540) 297-6066

Open: First weekend in March–December 1

Individual sites: 50

Each site has: Picnic table, fire grill, and lantern post

Site assignment: First come, first served

Registration: By reservation, (800) 933-PARK; or on arrival

Facilities: Telephone, soda machine, outside cold-water showers, water, and vault toilets

Parking: One vehicle per site, others at overflow parking area at entrance to campground

Fee: $14 per night

Elevation: 920 feet

Restrictions:

Pets—Must be kept caged or on a leash shorter than six feet; $3 fee per night

Fires—In grills and fire pits only

Alcoholic beverages—Public use or display is prohibited

Vehicles—Up to 50 feet

Other—Maximum 14-day stay in a 30-day period; no more than six people, two tents per site; swimming in beach area only; 10 p.m. to 8 a.m. quiet hours

STAUNTON RIVER STATE PARK

Scottsburg

CAMPGROUND RATINGS

Beauty: ★★★
Site privacy: ★★
Site spaciousness: ★★
Quiet: ★★★
Security: ★★★★
Cleanliness/upkeep: ★★★★

While Occoneechee State Park may be the first choice for boaters and fishermen, the seclusion that Staunton River offers is well worth the 45-minute drive from Occoneechee.

Staunton River State Park is located on a peninsula upstream from Occoneechee State Park at the narrow end of Buggs Island Lake, also known as the John H. Kerr Reservoir. The park and adjacent river are named for pre–Revolutionary War commander Captain Henry Staunton, whose contingent of soldiers kept early settlers safe from Indian attacks. This section of the Dan River became known as Captain Dan's River and later the Staunton River. It became an important route for transporting tobacco from the large plantations that were built in this southernmost section of Virginia. Sad to say, however, most were destroyed during the Civil War. This 1,597-acre park was another of the original six in Virginia's fledgling system, with many of the buildings constructed by the Civilian Conservation Corps from 1933–1935. Kerr Dam's opening in 1952 created the 48,000-acre Buggs Island Lake.

While Occoneechee State Park may be the first choice for boaters and fishermen, the seclusion that Staunton River offers is well worth the 45-minute drive from Occoneechee. VA 344 forms the main park road before terminating at the end of the peninsula. Shortly after passing the contact station, you'll see the sign for Staunton River's Campground on the left. Turn in here and enter the intimate figure eight over which the 48 sites are spread with a bathhouse in the center. Fourteen of these

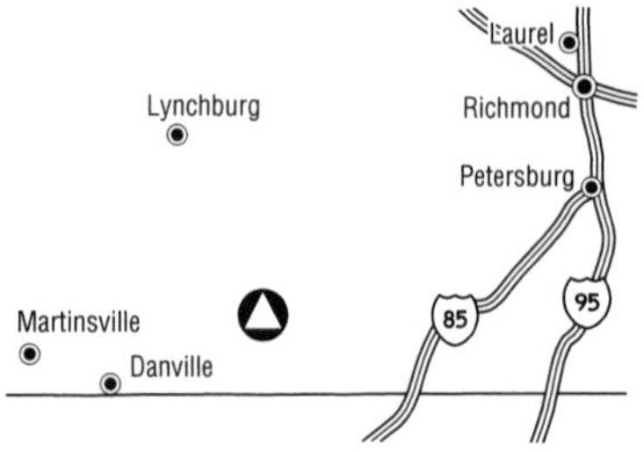

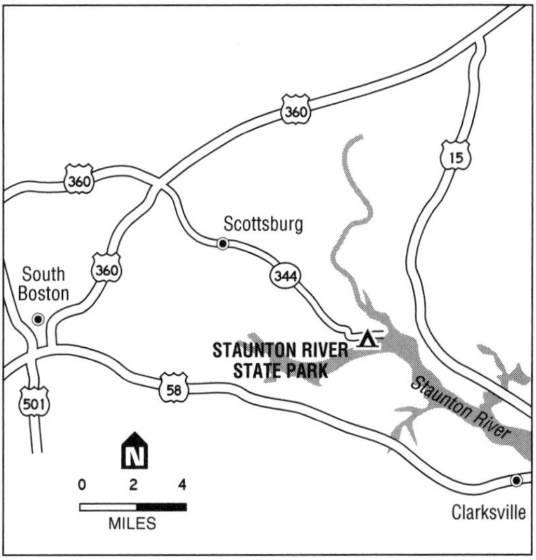

are standard sites sans electric and water hookups, so when things get busy you're likely to have RVs for neighbors, or maybe not. The campground lies in a wooded enclave of oak and pine trees that provides a modicum of shade.

However, chances are you'll spend little time in your tent when the sun's shining. Besides the aforementioned boating and fishing opportunities that attract many to Buggs Island Lake, bikers, hikers, and equestrians alike will enjoy the 7.5-mile River Bank Multi-Use Trail. The trail is an easy to moderate route that circumnavigates the 1,597-acre peninsula that's bounded by the Staunton and Dan Rivers as well as Buggs Island Lake and offers excellent water views. It's part of a recent concerted effort by the Virginia Department of Conservation and Recreation to accommodate a more diverse group of users, particularly mountain bikers. Other shorter trails range from 0.1 to 0.7 mile and serve to connect the park's main road with the River Bank Trail and other park facilities.

Although swimming from the park's shoreline is not allowed, you'll be able to take a dip in the park's swimming pool after working up a sweat while playing tennis or mountain biking. The little ones will enjoy playground facilities located near the pool and tennis courts. Or enjoy a leisurely paddle on the surrounding waters in your canoe or one you rent from River Traders just west of the entrance to the park. Birders and non-birders alike will appreciate the bird checklist compiled over 20 years by Jeffrey Blalock. This list is available in the park office and lists the frequency of sightings by seasons.

If you're interested in taking a historical side trip outside the park you may want to visit the nearby Staunton River Battlefield State Park, where makeshift Confederate troops of old men and young boys managed to hold off 5,000 Union troops at a strategic bridge over the Staunton River. The 300-acre battlefield includes a modern visitor center and self-guided walking trail that offer additional information about this historic site.

To get there: From US 58 along the southern border of Virginia, follow US 360 east for 18 miles from South Boston. Turn right and continue 10 miles on VA 344 to the park entrance.

KEY INFORMATION

Staunton River State Park
1170 Staunton Trail
Scottsburg, VA 24589

Operated by: Virginia Department of Conservation and Recreation

Information: (804) 572-4623

Open: First weekend in March–December 1

Individual sites: 48

Each site has: Picnic table and fire ring

Site assignment: First come, first served

Registration: By phone, (800) 933-PARK; or on arrival

Facilities: Bathhouse with flush toilets and hot showers, drink machine, and pay telephone

Parking: At campsites and day-use areas

Fee: $14 per night/$18 with electricity and water

Elevation: 370 feet

Restrictions:

Pets—Must be kept caged or kept on a leash shorter than six feet; $3 fee per night

Fires—Must be confined to camp stove or fire ring

Alcoholic beverages—Public use or display is prohibited

Vehicles—No limit

Other—Quiet hours 10 p.m. to 6 a.m.; length of stay no more than 14 consecutive days in a 30-day period; no more than six people, two tents, and two vehicles allowed per site

OCCONEECHEE STATE PARK

Clarksville

The 48,000-acre John H. Kerr Reservoir, also known as Buggs Island Lake, is Virginia's largest lake and the main attraction at Occoneechee State Park, which hugs the lake's shoreline in the shadow of the Virginia–North Carolina boundary. Boaters and fishermen alike flock to this lake, which is well known for the quantity and size of its largemouth bass, bluegill, crappie, and perch.

Occoneechee State Park is named for the Native American tribe that inhabited an island in the Roanoke River near the park's present location from 1250 until the late 1600s. Although the Occoneechee were quite friendly toward European settlers, they were massacred by Virginia Councilman Nathaniel Bacon and a group of men from Henrico County. To their credit, Governor Berkeley and the colonial government rebuked Bacon's brutal and misguided actions. Descendants of the Occoneechee celebrate their ancestors every May at the park with a Native American Festival and Powwow. Those interested in more information about the Native American presence should plan a stop at the park's new visitor center with its excellent informational display of the Occoneechee heritage and customs. William Towne established the 3,105-acre Occoneechee plantation on this site in 1839. As with many plantations, this was a virtually self-sustaining village until

CAMPGROUND RATINGS

Beauty: ★★★★
Site privacy: ★★★★
Site spaciousness: ★★★★
Quiet: ★★★
Security: ★★★★
Cleanliness/upkeep: ★★★★

Park designers creatively arranged the tent camping area to maximize privacy and excellent waterfront vistas.

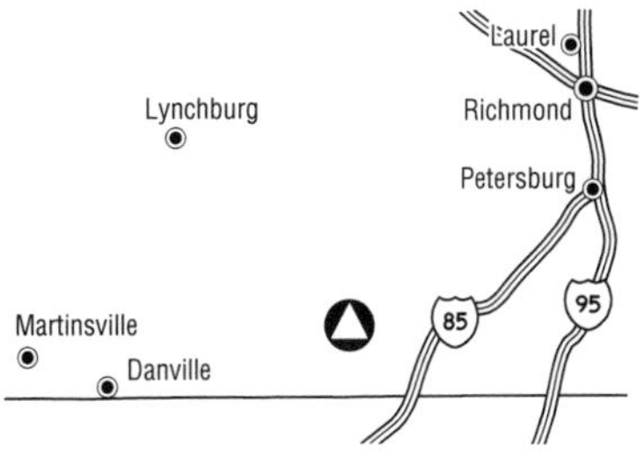

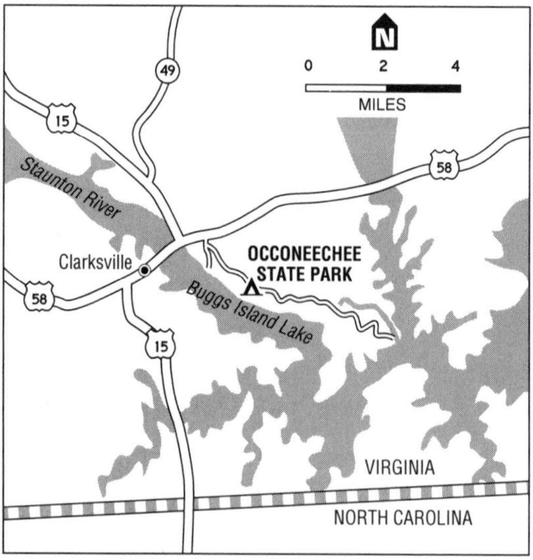

Townes's death in 1876, when the property was divided among his children and slaves. Eventually the mansion was sold outside the family and burned to the ground in 1898.

After leaving US 58 to enter the park, you'll drive down VA 364, the park's main road. Turn left after the contact station and continue a short distance until you reach campground B on the right-hand side. There are 88 sites spread out over Campgrounds B and C. In case you're wondering, as I was, the adjacent Occoneechee Wildlife Management Area took over what was formerly campground A. Campground B is divided with 52 sites designated for tent camping and the rest at an adjacent site with hookups for RVs.

Park designers creatively arranged the tent camping area to maximize privacy and excellent waterfront vistas. As you drive around the outer tent camping loop looking for a good space, look for one of the many numbered B31–B46 that offer this ideal combination. Many of the best sites are a short walk from their respective parking areas and set into the hillsides overlooking the lake or dense woods of oak, pine, and cedar. Tent camping sites at campground B generally offer excellent separation between each other and better than average distance from the road.

Continuing down the park road you'll come to the entrance to campground C on the right after you pass the 0.8-mile Big Oak Nature Trail. Many of the 35 sites located along dual loops on a small peninsula offer electric and water hookups and are located fairly close together. Campground C is more RV-oriented and would be a second choice to tent campers looking for quiet and privacy.

Besides the great fishing and boating that the John H. Kerr Reservoir has to offer, campers can enjoy a leisurely walk along the park's color-blazed trail system located between the contact station and entrance road to campground B. The trails range in length from the 1.2-mile Old Plantation Interpretive Trail to the 0.2-mile Warriors Path Nature Trail. Their degree of difficulty increases only as they dip and climb through riparian ravines. The park also offers picnic areas with excellent waterfront vistas; however, there is no swimming allowed from the park's shoreline.

To get there: From I-85, take the exit for US 58 just south of South Hill. Drive for 20 miles until spotting the entrance for the park about 1 mile east of Clarksville.

KEY INFORMATION

Occoneechee State Park
1192 Occoneechee Park Road
Clarksville, VA 23927

Operated by: Virginia Department of Conservation and Recreation

Information: (804) 374-2210

Open: First weekend in March–December 1

Individual sites: 88

Each site has: Picnic table, fire grill, and lantern pole

Site assignment: On arrival as available

Registration: By phone, (800) 933-PARK; or on arrival

Facilities: Bathhouse with flush toilets and hot showers

Parking: At campsites, trailheads, and boat landing

Fee: $14 per night; $18 with electric and water

Elevation: 350 feet

Restrictions:

Pets—Must kept in an enclosed area or on a leash shorter than six feet; $3 fee per night

Fires—Confined to camp stove or fire ring

Alcoholic beverages—Public use or display is prohibited

Vehicles—Up to 30 feet

Other—Length of stay no more than 14 days in a 30-day period; maximum of six people per campsite

NORTHERN CAMPGROUNDS

PRINCE WILLIAM FOREST PARK

Triangle

If your perception of northern Virginia is traffic gridlock, rampant development, and trees as endangered species, then Prince William Forest Park may very well cause an abrupt mind-shift. The truth is that this 17,000-acre woodland, located just 32 miles from the nation's capital, could just as easily be 32 miles from the middle of nowhere. Once you've gotten to the Oak Ridge Campground in the northwestern corner of the park, the thoughts and sounds of I-95 shadowing the park's entrance on the eastern edge will have long since drifted away.

The park's history dates back thousands of years to those days when Algonquin-speaking Native Americans hunted, fished, and farmed here prior to the arrival of the first European settlers in 1607. Since then, this Chesapeake Bay watershed has seen expansive tobacco cultivation and pyrite mining before benefiting from Civilian Conservation Corps labor and gaining National Park status in 1940. Although developed for recreational usage and watershed protection, the park became home to the Office of Strategic Services, precursor to the Central Intelligence Agency, during World War II. In 1948, it reverted to public use and remains the largest area of piedmont forest in the National Park system.

After leaving I-95 at exit 150, follow the signs a short distance to the park's entrance. Stop by the visitor center, pick up a map of

CAMPGROUND RATINGS

Beauty: ★★★★
Site privacy: ★★★★
Site spaciousness: ★★★★
Quiet: ★★★★
Security: ★★★★
Cleanliness/upkeep: ★★★

This 17,000-acre woodland, located just 32 miles from the nation's capital, could just as easily be 32 miles from the middle of nowhere.

NORTH

the park, and take in the exhibit explaining the rich history and natural history of Prince William Forest Park before heading off to the Oak Ridge Campground. The campground is 5.5 miles from the visitor center along the paved Scenic Drive. Plan to have $10 per night camping fee in exact change ready so that once you've pitched your tent, you're good to go. Once you've made it to this oasis, you'll not want to use your car again until it's time to go.

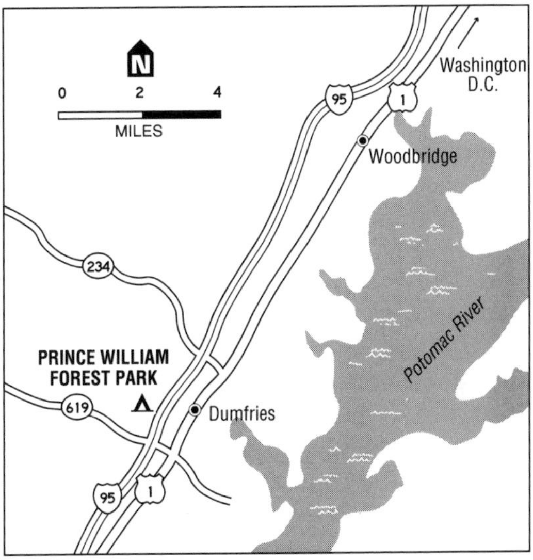

The Oak Ridge Campground consists of three loops, A–C, with nary a hookup, nor shower for that matter, among the 80 sites. RV'ers will have gone off to Travel Trailer Village, so you're not likely to be running up against somebody's Minnie Winnie. It says a lot about the park's commitment to environmental protection that campers are discouraged from collecting firewood in the interest of providing wildlife habitat and rebuilding topsoil. In the course of camping all over the Old Dominion, I have not seen another park that advocated this practice.

The overall terrain is rolling, but the campground itself is flat, heavily wooded with second-growth oaks and some small pines, and very private. Sites vary in size from spacious in loops A and B to the extremely spacious walk-in sites in loop C. And on top of that, the park's literature says the campground rarely fills up. Although there are probably those who use this campground as a relatively inexpensive way to explore Washington, my feeling is it's just too beautiful and natural a setting to park and drive away. And there are several northern Virginia campgrounds that are closer to D.C. that would serve as better base camps.

Opportunities for bikers and hikers abound at this park, so once you've settled into your site at Prince William Forest Park, just leave your car until it's time to go home. Some 37 miles of well-blazed hiking trails wind through the beech, holly, and oak forest with varied length and degree of difficulty, but the best place to start might be the 1-mile Farms to Forest loop Trail (with a possible 2.7-mile extension possible) which begins right at the campground entrance. From the 0.2-mile Pine Grove Forest Trail to the 9.7-mile South Valley Trail, there's something for anyone who wants to take a walk in the woods.

The park is also bicycle-friendly, whether you're on a road or mountain bike. The 7.5-mile paved Scenic Loop includes a 3.5-mile section of separate bike lanes from parking lot D to the Oak Ridge Campground. In addition, there are 16 miles of fire roads for mountain bikers that are rated from easy to difficult. However, the trails are closed to bicycles, so many of these fire roads are out-and-back rides. Be sure to pick up a copy of the bicycling guide for additional information.

Whether you're looking for a respite from the hectic pace of northern Virginia or a wooded destination at which to spend a few days, you'll find your time at Prince William Forest Park to be absolutely rejuvenating.

To get there: From I-95, take exit 150 and follow the signs less than 1 mile to the park's entrance.

KEY INFORMATION

Prince William Forest Park
P.O. Box 209
Triangle, VA 22172-0209

Operated by: National Park Service

Information: (703) 221-7181

Open: Year-round

Individual sites: 80

Each site has: Picnic table, grill, and lantern pole

Site assignment: First come, first served

Registration: Self-registration on site

Facilities: Water, flush toilets, and pay phone at visitor center

Parking: Two vehicles per site, additional vehicles park at campground entrance

Fee: $4 entry fee/$10 camping fee

Elevation: 350 feet

Restrictions:

Pets—Must be on leash shorter than six feet

Fires—Must be in grills; use provided firewood, leave down wood for wildlife

Alcoholic beverages—Allowed at campsite

Vehicles—Up to 33 feet

Other—Quiet hours 10 p.m. to 6 a.m.; sites in loops A and B are limited to two tents and six people, C loop sites are limited to four people; 14-day stay limit; skateboards, rollerblades, fireworks, and weapons are prohibited

POHICK BAY REGIONAL PARK

Lorton

"Pohick" was the name given this area by Algonquin Indians to aptly describe it as the "water place." With its marina, boat launch, and boat storage facilities, Pohick Bay Regional Park offers a year-round haven for boaters looking for access to the Potomac River, just 25 miles south of Washington, D.C., in Fairfax County. Those without a boat can choose from the park's rental fleet of pedal boats, sailboats, and jon boats. However, even landlubbers will find its 150 campsites a great place to sleep under the trees while leaving northern Virginia's traffic jams behind.

After entering the park from Gunston Road, you'll turn right and follow the signs to reach the camping area. Once you reach the camp center and store, continue straight to reach sites 1–100 with hookups or go left for 101–150 sans electricity. Both spots offer flat sites in a nicely wooded area laden with pine, beech, and holly trees. Sites 31–38 form a small loop at the back of a much larger loop composed of the remaining sites with electricity. These encircle a grassy playing field and, for the most part, offer a considerable degree of privacy and separation from each other. This is one of those situations in which you should not automatically eschew those sites with hookups because you wouldn't be using them. In some cases, you might find them to be very desirable depending

CAMPGROUND RATINGS

Beauty: ★★★
Site privacy: ★★★
Site spaciousness: ★★★
Quiet: ★★★
Security: ★★★
Cleanliness/upkeep: ★★★

Even landlubbers will find these 150 campsites a great place to sleep under the trees while leaving northern Virginia's traffic jams behind.

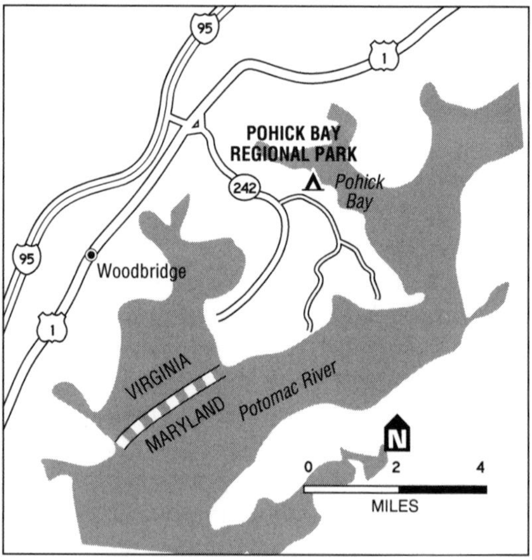

on how busy the park is. If you decide to go this route, try to get one of sites 31–38 located at the back on the small loop.

The sites without electric hookups are located a short distance away on the opposite side of the park's disc golf course and "giant" (their word, not mine) swimming pool. These are also laid out on a large and small loop in a more contained but heavily wooded area. Sites 101–150 generally appeared smaller than 1–100 with more understory between sites, so the privacy issue is probably a wash. Should you camp in the nonelectric area, try to get one of sites 103–120, which are pretty spacious and offer a good deal of privacy. Weekends and holidays are particularly busy times at Pohick, especially given its emphasis on boating activities, so try to plan a mid-week outing if solitude and quiet are high on your priority list.

Municipal parks such as Pohick Bay Regional Park by necessity take a different approach to outdoor recreation than the state and federal campgrounds listed in this guide. The recreational needs of more than three million northern Virginians create a different model than a remote campground in the mountains to the west. There are probably those purists who would dismiss camping in a facility that also features 18-hole golf and Frisbee golf courses, expansive playing fields, and boating facilities. However, everybody is entitled to their own definition of back to nature, and northern Virginians shouldn't have to spend the better part of a weekend driving to find a campsite when they've got some pretty dandy ones right in their own backyard.

If you're looking for more nature-oriented activities to enjoy during your stay at Pohick, plan to take a short drive down the road to Mason Neck State Park. The park and wildlife refuge teem with the flora and fauna that are unique to wetlands habitat, including more than 200 species of birds. You'll see the more than 1,000 pairs of great blue herons in their rookery, a scene that appears almost prehistoric as these massive birds gently flap through the air with their necks bent and croak at each other. However, it's the 15–50 bald eagles that frequent the park at any given time that attracts many birding enthusiasts. Walk along the shoreline trail or take a half-day guided canoe trip to get a really good glimpse of the area's natural features.

To get there: From I-95, take the Lorton exit. Turn left onto Lorton Road, right onto US 1, and then left onto Gunston Road. Continue past the golf course to the park entrance on the left.

KEY INFORMATION

Pohick Bay Regional Park
6501 Pohick Bay Drive
Lorton, VA 22709

Operated by: Northern Virginia Regional Park Authority

Information: (703) 339-6104

Open: Year-round

Individual sites: 150

Each site has: Picnic table and grill

Site assignment: First come, first served

Registration: By reservation or on site

Facilities: Camp store, laundry, soda machine, telephone, water, and showers

Parking: At campsite and swimming pool

Fee: $12 per night/ $15 for electric sites

Elevation: 50 feet

Restrictions:

Pet—Must be on leash shorter than six feet

Fires—Confine to camp stove and fire ring

Alcoholic beverages—Prohibited

Vehicles—Up to 33 feet

Other—Seven-day maximum stay

BURKE LAKE PARK

Fairfax Station

Entering Burke Lake Park from Ox Road in Fairfax County, the first impression that you'll first have is from the park's 18-hole golf course and driving range. However, keep driving as the park's main road winds around past the 218-acre lake before reaching the campground entrance located next to the maintenance area. An alternate, albeit less picturesque entrance to the campground, is via Burke Lake Road.

The campground's 140 sites, none with electrical hookups, are spread out among three areas noted as A, B, and C. There is a noticable difference among sites, and campers would be wise to drive or walk through the campground to choose a site if possible. For most of us who crave a little privacy in the woods, sites B1–16 are going to be the most appealing with those numbered 4, 6, 8, and 10 at the top of the list since they appeared to be the most private and bordered in back by the park's five-mile trail.

Someone had long since given up on the idea of growing any vegetation under the trees in C, so all that remains is a gravel base. As a result, those sites in Family Camping Area C, although individually numbered, were hard to distinguish from each other or, for that matter, from the gravel roads that loop throughout this section of the 883-acre park. There are also some appealing sites in Area A, but these

CAMPGROUND RATINGS

Beauty: ★★★
Site privacy: ★★★
Site spaciousness: ★★★
Quiet: ★★
Security: ★★★
Cleanliness/upkeep: ★★★

Don't think that you need to jump back into your vehicle after setting up your campsite to find something to do.

NORTH

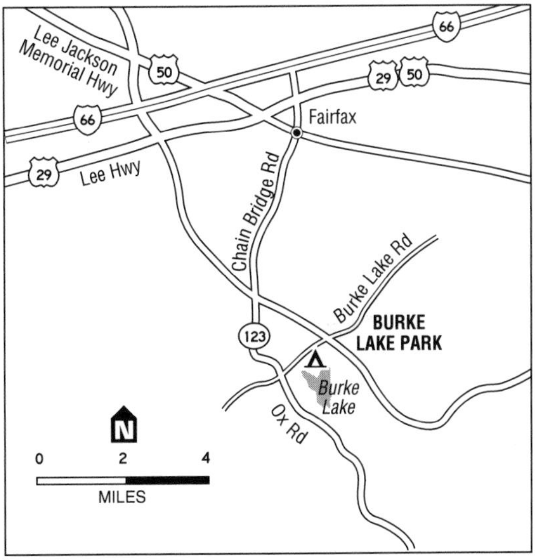

are in close proximity to the group camping area and the entrance road to the campground, allowing the possibilty for somewhat noisy conditions. Groups of seven or more campers can use the "wilderness camping," which will get you as far into the woods as possible at Burke Lake Park. However, note that the wilderness camping area is primitive and lacks both water and bathroom facilities. The wilderness area includes an orienteering course laid out for both beginners and advanced map and compass users.

The beauty of camping at northern Virginia campgrounds like Burke Lake is not so much the ability to "rough it" but more the opportunity to sleep outdoors with all of the recreational, cultural, and educational activities that this vast suburb of Washington, D.C., has to offer. However, don't think that you need to jump back into your vehicle after setting up your campsite to find something to do. Therein lies the key to enjoying this facility managed by the Fairfax County Park Authority.

The lake itself offers a myriad of possibilities. Whether you bring your own canoe or rent a boat on site, you're sure to enjoy exploring Burke Lake's interesting coves as well as the waterfowl refuge on Vesper Island, which lies within its boundaries. Gasoline motors and sailboats are not allowed on the lake, however. Many northern Virginian fishermen come to the lake to cast a line for largemouth bass, walleye, muskie, catfish, crappie, perch, and bluegill. Bait and tackle are available at the park's marina or bring your own. Virginia fishing licenses are required.

Picnic areas with shelters for rent, an 18-hole par-three golf course, driving range, Frisbee golf course, a miniature railroad, five-mile walking trail, 18-station fitness trail, sand volleyball courts, playing fields, and even an ice cream parlor round out the kinds of activities that you'll find at this island of green amid the sprawling developments of northern Virginia. Be sure to leave your cellular phone and laptop at home, and you're guaranteed to have as much outdoor fun as possible within such a short distance to Washington.

To get there: From the I-495 Beltway, take exit 5 onto Braddock Road. Go west on Braddock Road and then turn left onto Ox Road. Drive a short distance until you see the park entrance on the left.

KEY INFORMATION

Burke Lake Park
7315 Ox Road
Fairfax Station, VA 22039

Operated by: Fairfax County Park Authority

Information: (703) 323-6600

Open: May through September

Individual sites: 140

Each site has: Picnic table and grill

Site assignment: First come, first served

Registration: On site

Facilities: Camp store, hot showers, water, and pay phone

Parking: Limited to one camping vehicle and one noncamping vehicle

Fee: $12 per night for first four people, $2 for each extra person

Elevation: 430 feet

Restrictions:

Pets—Must be on leash

Fires—Wood fires in ring only; charcoal fire in grill

Alcoholic beverages—Prohibited

Vehicles—Up to 25 feet

Other—Seven-day maximum stay; quiet time 10 p.m. to 7 a.m.; all campers must use a camper, tent, or other camping device

LAKE FAIRFAX PARK

Reston

Lake Fairfax Park's 476 wooded and open acres are tucked away into a pretty high-end neighborhood, even for northern Virginia. I noticed a sign in a newly built adjacent subdivision advertising homes "Starting from $795,000." While it's hard to put a value on outdoor recreation, that figure does help bring the cost of property into an exaggerated perspective near the nation's capital. Once you've plunked down that kind of change for a roof over your head, it's nice to know that there are green spaces nearby for some R & R.

The first thing you'll notice as you enter the park is the fairly new Water Mine: Family Swimming Hole. Taking its lead from Water Country and other aquatic playgrounds, the Water Mine includes Pete's Peak, water flumes, Rattlesnake River, Box Canyon Crossing, and for small children, the Tenderfoot Pond. Some of you may scoff at this obvious commercialism when coupled with camping; but families with kids who are trying to break into the camping experience will find that the Water Mine makes the experience a lot more fun. And in the summer, most of us will find the water attraction downright refreshing, especially since swimming is not allowed in the lake.

Driving into the park, you'll notice a more natural environment with tree-lined streams alongside the road, which climbs to the hilltop campground. You will also

CAMPGROUND RATINGS

Beauty: ★★★
Site privacy: ★★★
Site spaciousness: ★★★
Quiet: ★★★
Security: ★★★
Cleanliness/upkeep: ★★★

Many families with young 'uns will find a lot to enjoy during the summer at Lake Fairfax Park.

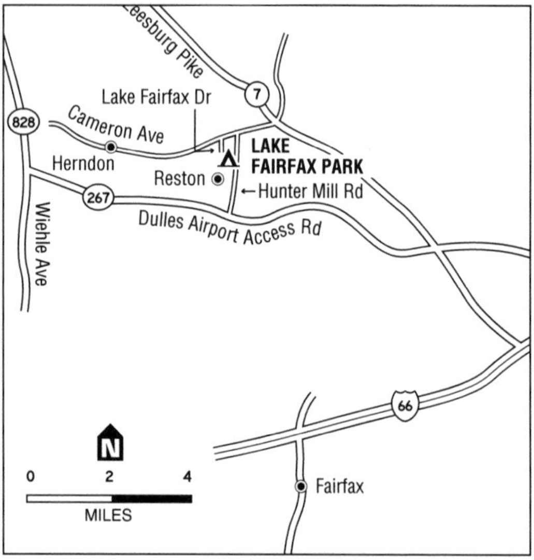

notice signs for the requisite ball fields like any other northern Virginia municipal park. In addition, this park offers a cricket field. After winding your way to the campground, you'll notice that all the campsites have electric hookups and many are in the open field with a few oak trees scatered about. However, along the wooded edge are a number of sites that would provide ample shade and privacy. Plan your arrival during the week and take a close look at sites 51, 53, 55, 57, 60, 62, 64, 66, 68, 70, 72, 74, 76, 77, and, my favorite, 78.

As I've mentioned with the other northern Virginia municipal campgrounds, camping at Fairfax Lake Park is not the ultimate back-to-nature experience that many of you think of in connection with camping; but it's pretty ideal for the family that is trying out tent camping while keeping a wide array of less woodsy entertainment close by. Other books have been written about all that there is to do in this vast suburb of Washington, D.C.; and, no doubt, many of you will find that Lake Fairfax Park is an ideal and relatively inexpensive place to stay while sightseeing around our nation's capital. However, you could just as easily leave your cellular telephone and laptop at home, park your car, and enjoy the park's activities without driving again until you've broken camp.

The park also includes a playground, carousel, short trails, and miniature train ride. In addition, you can fish and rent pedal boats to laze around the 18-acre lake. You can fish for panfish in the lake or stocked trout in the stream that courses through the park. There is even a free children's entertainment series that is held on Saturdays throughout the summer. Undoutedly, Lake Fairfax Park offers a different sort of camping and outdoor experience than most others in this guide. But this is northern Virginia, and I think that many families with young `uns will find a lot to enjoy during the summer at Lake Fairfax Park.

To get there: From the I-495 Beltway, take exit 10B and go 6.5 miles west on Leesburg Pike. Turn left onto Baron Cameron Avenue and then left onto Lake Fairfax Drive. The park entrance is a short distance ahead on the left.

KEY INFORMATION

Lake Fairfax Park
1400 Lake Fairfax Drive
Reston, VA 20190

Operated by: Fairfax County Park Authority

Information: (703) 324-8702

Open: March 1–December 1

Individual sites: 136

Each site has: Picnic table, grill, and electricity

Site assignment: As available

Registration: By reservation, (703) 471-5415; (703) 757-9242 from May through September

Facilities: Bathhouse with hot showers and flush toilets, water, and camp store

Parking: Limited to one vehicle in addition to camping unit

Fee: $12 per night, $15 with hookups

Elevation: 520 feet

Restrictions:

Pets—Must be on leash and attended at all times

Fires—Confine to camp stove, grill, or fireplace

Alcoholic beverages—Prohibited

Vehicles—No limit

Other—Seven-day maximum stay; quiet time 10 p.m. to 7 a.m.; all campers must use a camper, tent, or other camping device

BULL RUN REGIONAL PARK

Centreville

Bull Run Regional Park offers many things to those looking for some fresh air and respite from gridlock. However, Civil War enthusiasts will readily identify Bull Run with the two battles fought at nearby Manassas National Battlefield Park. Touring information can be found at the park's Visitor Center located on VA 234, which includes a bookstore offering an extensive array of Civil War titles. You can also pick up a battlefield map that details the various trails, roads, and sites that were part of First Manassas (First Bull Run) in July of 1861 and Second Manassas (Second Bull Run) in August of 1862.

You can follow the mile-long self-guided walking tour of Henry Hill to see the First Manassas Battlefield. Located behind the Visitor Center, the tour uses taped messages and signage to explain what occurred during this early clash between Confederate and Union troops on July 21, 1861. Union troops expected to take this strategic railroad junction and put an early end to the war. Such was the atmosphere of optimism that citizens and Congressmen from the capital arrived at the site, literally prepared for a picnic. This was not to be an easy victory, and Confederate troops drove the Union soldiers back into Washington by 4 p.m., causing a chaotic situation as the retreating army got tangled up with sightseers. It

CAMPGROUND RATINGS

Beauty:	★★★
Site privacy:	★★★★
Site spaciousness:	★★★
Quiet:	★★★
Security:	★★★★
Cleanliness/upkeep:	★★★★

Civil War enthusiasts will readily identify Bull Run with the two battles fought at nearby Manassas National Battlefield Park.

NORTH

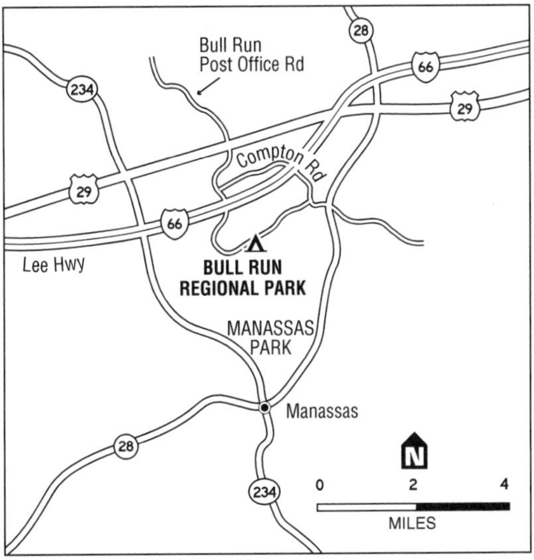

was here that General Thomas J. Jackson received his nickname, "Stonewall."

Thirty miles of hiking trails and 20 miles of bridle paths lace the 4,500-acre Manassas Battlefield. There is no connection between Bull Run Regional Park and the National Battlefield Park except proximity, but camping at Bull Run is a great way to gain access to this fascinating piece of U.S. and Virginia Civil War history.

Be sure to stop in the town of Manassas, especially at the Visitor Center located in a newly renovated train depot. A fascinating walking or driving tour of Old Town Manassas starts at the depot. In this designated Main Street Community, you'll find a wide selection of fine restaurants, art studios, galleries, and antique shops, as well as the Manassas Volunteer Fire Company Museum.

After entering Bull Run Drive from the intersection of Bull Run Post Office and Compton Roads, you'll pass through a sparse residential neighborhood before reaching the park's entrance. The drone of I-66 will have wafted off into the background after driving two more miles to reach the campground. Along the way, you'll get an idea of the park's other offerings, including picnic shelters, miniature and Frisbee golf courses, soccer fields, a large swimming pool, and a shooting center featuring skeet, archery, and a sporting clay course. The expansive, grassy playing fields and sycamore trees on the park's 1,500 flat acres bordering Cub Run and Bull Run suggest a flood plain—but the campground is located on higher ground with its own emergency access, so high water is generally not a problem.

The heavily wooded campground is located near the center of the park. Sites are well-spaced, private, and flat, and they are spread out along a large loop with three smaller inner loops. A third of the 150 sites are non-electric, and these are located along the outer edge of the campground loop. While campers may have particular preferences on arrival, the combination of dense oak woods, understory, and ample size and spacing of campsites is such that you'll have a hard time finding fault with any of the nonelectric sites. Municipal parks such as this must be many things to many people, but Bull Run's ability to provide such a pleasant back-to-the-woods camping experience within a stone's throw of I-66 and 25 miles from Washington, D.C., is nothing short of amazing. The park readily fills up on holiday weekends as well as in early spring, when Bull Run's famous bluebells are in bloom. Reservations are strongly recommended at all times.

Nature trails traverse the area, but hikers and equestrians looking for an extended outing will head for the 17.5-mile (point-to-point) Bull Run Occoquan Trail, whose trailhead is located near the campground entrance. Winding along the Occoquan Reservoir through 4,000 acres of riparian woodlands, this linear trail passes Hemlock Overlook Park and Bull Run Marina before reaching its terminus at Fountainhead Park. Be sure to pick up a trail brochure for more information before starting out.

To get there: From I-66, take exit 52 at Centreville and go 2 miles north on US 29 to Bull Run Post Office Road. Follow signs to the park entrance at a sharp bend to the left.

KEY INFORMATION

Bull Run Regional Park
7700 Bull Run Drive
Centreville, VA 22020

Operated by: Northern Virginia Regional Park Authority

Information: (703) 631-0550

Open: First Saturday in March through mid-November

Individual sites: 150

Each site has: Picnic table, grill, and campfire ring

Site assignment: First come, first served

Registration: By reservation or on arrival

Facilities: Camp store, laundry, bathhouses with hot showers, pay phone, and water

Parking: At campsites

Fee: $4.50 entry fee for first nine people plus $ 12.50 per night/$15.75 with electric camping fee

Elevation: 160 feet

Restrictions:

Pets—Must be attended and on leash

Fires—Wood fires only within ground ring; only charcoal in grills; all fires must be attended

Alcoholic beverages—Prohibited

Vehicles—Up to 45 feet

Other—Quiet hours 10 p.m. to 7 a.m.; cutting of trees and collecting downed wood is prohibited; all campers must use a camper, tent, or other camping device; maximum stay of seven consecutive days

WESTERN CAMPGROUNDS

MATHEWS ARM CAMPGROUND

Luray

Shenandoah National Park was formally dedicated on July 3, 1936, by President Franklin D. Roosevelt. Its 194,600 acres are closer to more people than any other national park, and roughly 1.8 million get on the 105-mile Skyline Drive to visit the park every year. There are entrances at Front Royal (mile 0), Thornton Gap (mile 31.5), Swift Run Gap (mile 65.7), and Rockfish Gap (mile 104.6). October weekends are, by far, the busiest times for visitation, and it's difficult to get one of the park's 647 campsites spread out among its four campgrounds. On the other hand, I found these same campgrounds to be almost empty during the week at the same time of year.

Mathews Arm is the northernmost campground in Shenandoah National Park. After pulling off the Skyline Drive at mile 22.2, you'll descend to the registration station. After passing the trailer dump station on the left and a parking area on the right, you'll enter the campground consisting of loops A–C. A modicum of privacy is provided by mature oak and hickory as well as the numerous rock outcrops that punctuate this area. Despite the uneven slope over much of Mathews Arm Campground, campsites are level; you'll have no trouble pitching your tent. Those sites closest to the entrance station are more open and will attract RVers despite the lack of any RV hookups. While there are many desirable

CAMPGROUND RATINGS

Beauty: ★★★★
Site privacy: ★★★★
Site spaciousness: ★★★★
Quiet: ★★★★
Security: ★★★★
Cleanliness/upkeep: ★★★★★

Despite the uneven slope over much of Mathews Arm Campground, campsites are level; you'll have no trouble pitching your tent.

WEST

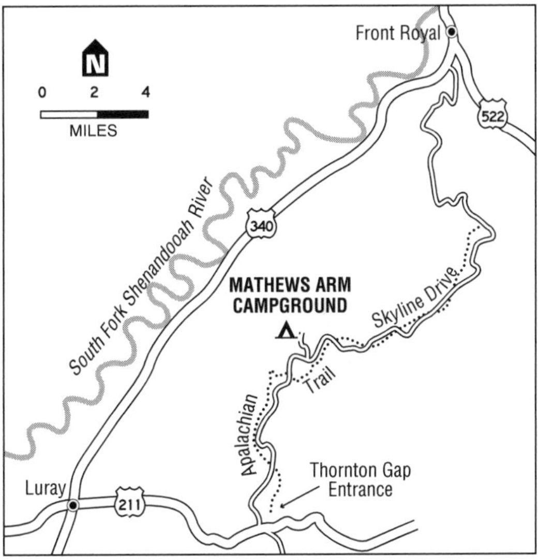

sites here, most are adjacent to one of the campground loop roads. However, at the back of the campground is the "Tents Only" area comprising sites B89–B102, which are more set off by themselves. You'll have to carry your gear a short distance from the central parking area, but the quiet and privacy back here make it well worth the small extra effort.

Opportunities for hiking abound with 95 miles of the 2,100-mile Appalachian Trail running through the park. Many through-hikers agree that the section of AT through Shenandoah National Park is the most beautiful of the trail's entire length from Georgia to Maine. Shenandoah also includes an additional 425 miles of trails, most of which connect to the Appalachian Trail. However, bicycles are not allowed on any trails within the park.

A population of some 5,000 whitetail deer resides within the park's boundaries, and you're sure to encounter them at some time during your visit. Keep in mind, however, that it's illegal to feed these or other park animals. An estimated 500–800 black bear also live within Shenandoah National Park. You should seriously heed park warnings to store your food in bear-proof containers, keep food out of your tent at least 100 yards away, and use park-provided bear-proof food storage poles or suspend food from trees at least 10 feet from the ground and 4 feet from either tree.

There are several pleasant trails adjacent to the campground. The 1.7-mile Traces Nature Trail is a fairly level loop circling Mathews Arm Campground and starts from the parking area by the campground's registration station. It also connects with the Mathews Arm Trail, a gated service road that starts at the end of the tents-only section. It proceeds largely downhill before intersecting with the Tuscarora-Overall Run Trail, which will take you down to the picturesque Overall Run Falls after a roughly two-mile walk. Staying on the entire 4.4-mile Mathews Arm Trail will lead you along Mathews Arm Ridge to the Shenandoah National Park boundary.

To get there: From the Thornton Gap entrance (mile 31.5) to Shenandoah National Park, drive north on the Skyline Drive to the entrance to Mathews Arm Campground at mile 22.2.

KEY INFORMATION

Mathews Arm Campground
Shenandoah National Park
3655 U.S. Highway 211 East
Luray, VA 22835-9036

Operated by: National Park Service

Information: (540) 999-3500

Individual sites: 179

Each site has: Picnic table and fire grill

Site assignment: First come, first served

Registration: On arrival

Facilities: Flush toilets

Parking: At campsite and near amphitheater

Fee: $14 per night plus $10 park entrance fee

Elevation: 2,800 feet

Restrictions:

Pets—Must be on leash shorter than six feet; clean up after pet; don't leave unattended

Fires—Only in camp stoves and fireplaces

Alcoholic beverages—Permitted

Vehicles—No limit

Other—Do not carve, chop, or damage any live trees; wash dishes at campsite, not at restrooms, but gray water must be disposed of in service sinks at restrooms; campsite capacity is six people, two tents, two vehicles per site; quiet hours 10 p.m. to 6 a.m.

BIG MEADOWS CAMPGROUND

Luray

Big Meadows is Shenandoah National Park's largest treeless area, now encompassing a barren plateau that is approximately 640 acres, reduced from 1,000 acres in 1900. It's thought that Native Americans may have cleared the area to create favorable grazing conditions. European settlers overgrazed this site with beef cattle, especially during the Civil War. Park officials have used a variety of means to prevent the growth of black locust and blackberry which would, in time, take over the meadow. Park Service officials used combinations of burning and mowing in an attempt to hold back the growth of certain invasive vegetation, but realized that the burning actually helped the locust and blackberry spread. New strategies have aided in the establishment of meadow grasses. Today the dominant shrub growth in the meadow is blueberry with swamp varieties such as marsh marigold, swamp fern, and Canadian burnet growing in wetter areas with some 270 species of vascular plants. In addition to the whitetail deer that wander seemingly carefree through the meadow, you're also likely to see song sparrows, meadowlarks, grouse, foxes, and skunks.

Besides its unique natural qualities, Big Meadows hosted the park's dedication on July 3, 1936. President Franklin D. Roosevelt himself was on hand to formally open the facilities at Shenandoah National Park.

CAMPGROUND RATINGS

Beauty: ★★★★
Site privacy: ★★★★
Site spaciousness: ★★★★
Quiet: ★★★★
Security: ★★★★
Cleanliness/upkeep: ★★★★★

In addition to the whitetail deer that wander seemingly carefree through the meadow, you're also likely to see song sparrows, meadowlarks, grouse, foxes, and skunks.

WEST

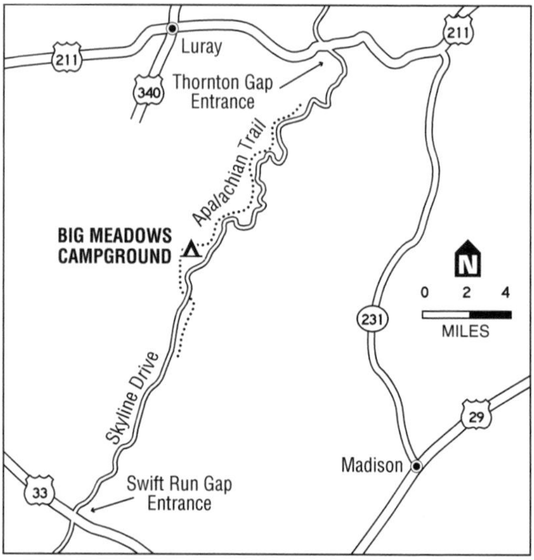

The meadow is located across the Skyline Drive from the Harry F. Byrd Visitor Center where you'll find informative exhibits, a library, auditorium, and an array of literature pertaining to Shenandoah National Park that is on sale.

Big Meadows with its visitor center, lodge, restaurant, and campground is located in the central section of the park at mile 51.3. After pulling off the Skyline Drive near the Byrd Visitor Center, follow the signs to the registration station for Big Meadows Campground. Its 217 sites are situated on two large loops, the front one comprising loops P–T and the rear section containing U–Y, which are designated as RV sites despite the lack of hookups.

Of the 178 non-RV sites, these can be divided into the 144 you can drive up to and the 35 designated as walk-in sites. The drive-in sites are spacious and generally offer considerable foliage to separate each other. Park officials did a good job of laying out so many sites while providing a certain amount of seclusion for each. However, this is, of course, relative; those of you who really relish your solitude will accept the slight inconvenience of walking 10–20 yards and opt for one of the walk-in sites.

The walk-in sites are set off in the wooded edge of Big Meadows Campground and are very private. Sites P4–P10 are set between the main entrance road and the camp road and would tend to be noiser than the others; but P29–40 and P44–53 are set off by themselves in the woods and will look mighty appealing. P12–21 and P24–34 are in grassy, and somewhat less heavily wooded areas but are still highly desirable if you don't mind the slight inconvenience of carrying your gear to the site. Big Meadows Campground is a very popular stopover for campers in Shenandoah National Park, especially in the fall; and it is the only one that accepts reservations. If you can plan your stay during the week, you'll find considerably fewer neighbors, but calling ahead is a good idea just to be on the safe side.

As in the rest of this nearly 300-square-mile park through which 95 miles of the famed Appalachian Trail passes, there is no shortage of hiking trails. However, the Big Meadows area is especially blessed with trails for hikers of varied age and ability levels. The 1.8-mile Story of the Forest Nature Trail is a relatively easy loop starting from the Byrd Visitor Center. You'll find interpretive signs that explain various aspects of the surrounding forest. The 3.8-mile Lewis Springs Falls Trail provides more of challenge in terms of length and change in elevation after it exits from the X section of the Big Meadows campground. The hike to the 81-foot falls is worth the effort.

Camp Hoover, located across from Big Meadows 6.3 miles down the Rapidan Fire Road, was a favorite get-away for President Herbert Hoover. The walk to Camp Hoover can be shortened to a 4-mile out-and-back by taking the Mill Prong Trail. Camp Hoover is a beautiful spot where 3 of the original 13 cabins remain at the confluence of Mill Prong, Laurel Prong, and the Rapidan River. The cabins are open for tours with a shuttle bus running back and forth from the Byrd Visitor Center on the weekend closest to President Hoover's August 10th birthday.

To get there: From the Swift Run Gap Entrance Station at mile 65.7, drive north on the Skyline Drive to Big Meadows at mile 51.3.

KEY INFORMATION

Big Meadows Campground
Shenandoah National Park
3655 U.S. Highway 211 East
Luray, VA 22835-9036

Operated by: National Park Service

Information: (540) 999-3500

Individual sites: 217

Each site has: Picnic table and fire grill

Site assignment: On arrival by camper

Registration: By advance reservation, (800) 365-CAMP; or on arrival

Facilities: Camp store, laundry, coin-operated showers, and lodge with restaurant

Parking: At campsites and across from entrance station

Fee: $17 plus $10 park entrance fee

Elevation: 3,500 feet

Restrictions:

Pets—Must be on leash shorter than six feet; clean up after pet; don't leave unattended

Fires—Only in camp stoves and fireplaces

Alcoholic beverages—Permitted

Vehicles—No limit

Other—Do not carve, chop, or damage any live trees; campsite capacity is six people, two tents, two vehicles per site; quiet hours 10 p.m. to 6 a.m.

LEWIS MOUNTAIN CAMPGROUND

Luray

Lewis Mountain Campground is located in the central section of Shenandoah National Park. With only 32 campsites, it's the smallest of the park's five campgrounds. Of these, half are designated as tent sites and half for RVs. There are no electric hookups, and this is the only campground in Shenandoah National Park that does not have sewage disposal tanks. If you're fortunate enough to snag a site at Lewis Mountain, you'll find a quiet, rustic setting that is sometimes overlooked in favor of the park's larger campgrounds.

After pulling off the Skyline Drive at milepost 57.5, you'll first pass through the Lewis Mountain picnic area and then continue past rental cabins before reaching the campground. The campground consists of one large loop with two smaller loops carved out among mature maple, pine, hemlock, and oak trees, with little vegetation to screen one campsite from another. Of the 32 sites, numbers 11, 14, 15, 16, and 18 are the more private. The tent pads are gravel, so a ground cloth and sleeping pad are highly recommended. It is not possible to reserve a site in advance, so at the busiest times, like autumn weekends, you won't be able to drive in and find yourself a site. As with the other Shenandoah National Park campgrounds, it's best to plan your arrival during the week, especially if you're coming to see the spectacular October leaf colors.

CAMPGROUND RATINGS

Beauty: ★★★★
Site privacy: ★★★
Site spaciousness: ★★★
Quiet: ★★★★
Security: ★★★★
Cleanliness/upkeep: ★★★★★

If you're fortunate enough to snag a site at Lewis Mountain, you'll find a quiet, rustic setting that is sometimes overlooked in favor of the park's larger campgrounds.

WEST

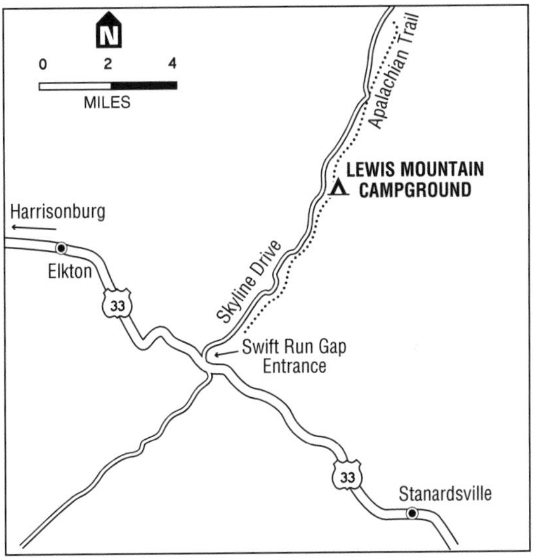

Upon your arrival to the campground, you'll be welcomed by a sign that reads, "Bear Country—Protect Your Property and Food—Proper Food Storage is Required." This is not an idle warning, and campers should use the food storage poles in the campground. It's especially important not to eat or store food in your tent lest you have unwanted late-night visitors of the large and furry kind.

This campground doesn't offer access to an abundance of hiking trails as do the park's other campgrounds. However, nowhere in Shenandoah National Park are you too far from the over 450 miles of trails that crisscross the 196,000-acre park. The half-mile (point-to-point) Lewis Mountain Trail departs from site 16 on its short ascent to Lewis Mountain via a mossy and fern-lined path. Numerous other hikes are accessible via the Appalachian Trail, which you can reach from site 3. Just as the 105-mile Skyline Drive forms the park's backbone for driving, 95 miles of the AT form a spine of sorts for hikers. Shenandoah's abundant side trails are just a short drive away.

Either by walking south along the Appalachian Trail or driving on the Skyline Drive to milepost 59.5, you can reach the start of the Pocosin Mission Trail. You'll pass one of the Potomac Appalachian Trail Cabins as you amble along the fire road to the site of an old Episcopal mission, established around 1904, complete with a fascinating, overgrown cemetery. Turn around and head back for a pretty easy 2.2-mile walk in the woods. Stretch this into a longer and more challenging 5.6-mile out-and-back by continuing on the yellow-blazed trail to Pocosin Hollow before returning.

Head north a short distance to milepost 56.4 to get onto the Bearfence Mountain Trail. You'll do your share of huffing and puffing as you scramble over the volcanic boulders, but by the time you reach the 3,640-foot summit of Bearfence Mountain, you'll enjoy a panoramic view that, on a clear day, will seem to go on forever. Backtrack or loop around for an approximate one-mile outing. Be sure to pick up one of the trail guides to Shenandoah Park that are listed in the appendix for a more complete selection of places to walk in the vicinity of Lewis Mountain Campground.

To get there: From the Swift Run Gap Entrance Station at mile 65.7 and US 33, drive north on the Skyline Drive to the campground entrance at mile 57.5.

KEY INFORMATION

Lewis Mountain Campground
Shenandoah National Park
3655 U.S. Highway 211 East
Luray, VA 22835-9036

Operated by: National Park Service

Information: (540) 999-3500

Open: Beginning of May through end of November

Individual sites: 32

Each site has: Picnic table and fire grill

Site assignment: Campers can choose from available sites

Registration: On arrival

Facilities: Camp store, laundry room, coin-operated showers, and flush toilets

Parking: At campsite and next to camp store

Fee: $14 in addition to $10 park entrance fee

Elevation: 3,396 feet

Restrictions:

Pets—Must be on leash shorter than six feet; clean up after pet; don't leave unattended

Fires—Only in camp stoves and fireplaces

Alcoholic beverages—Permitted

Vehicles—Up to 30 feet on pull-through sites

Other—Do not carve, chop, or damage any live trees; campsite capacity is six people, two tents, two vehicles per site; quiet hours 10 p.m. to 6 a.m.

LOFT MOUNTAIN CAMPGROUND

Luray

Loft Mountain Campground is located just off the Skyline Drive in the southern section of Shenandoah National Park at mile 79.5. It's unique among the park's other campgrounds in that it's located at the top of the mountain, and as a result there are great panoramic views of the neighboring peaks, valley, and piedmont from this 3,400-foot perch. Another unique feature at Loft Mountain Campground, which actually sits atop Big Flat Mountain, is the absence of mature, lofty hardwoods which you get accustomed to enjoying in Shenandoah National Park. They've been replaced by an abundance of thick, low-growing shrubbery, which offers a considerable degree of privacy between campsites. This mountaintop was once pastureland, but the present dense vegetation diminishes the feeling of being crowded at a campground that contains 219 sites. Loft Mountain Campground is the southernmost of Shenandoah's campgrounds and makes an excellent base from which to explore this end of the national park.

The campground consists of Loop A, which circumscribes the entire campground with the smaller loops B–H cutting across the center of loop A. The majority of the sites are private and spacious, but those who want to fully enjoy the feeling of being off by themselves should look first at the 54 "walk-in" sites located on the outer edge of

CAMPGROUND RATINGS

Beauty: ★★★★
Site privacy: ★★★★
Site spaciousness: ★★★★
Quiet: ★★★★
Security: ★★★★
Cleanliness/upkeep: ★★★★★

There are great panoramic views of the neighboring peaks, valley, and piedmont from this 3,400-foot perch.

WEST

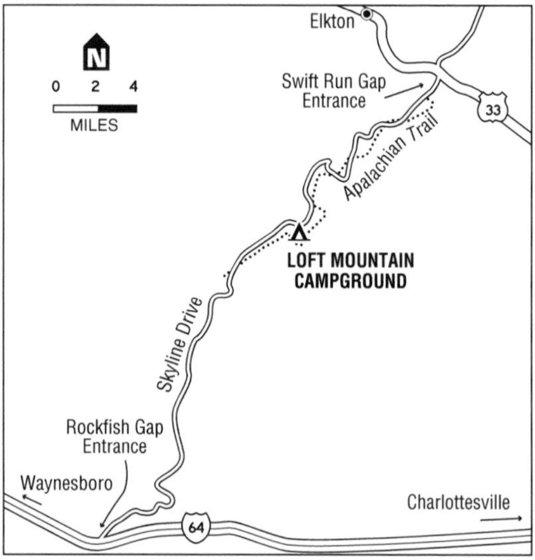

loop A. Parking is nearby and reserved for each site, but you'll have to carry your gear a short distance to your home in the woods which includes a picnic table, grill, and tent site.

Fall weekends are the most popular times for camping here as well as the rest of Shenandoah National Park, and sites are available on a first-come, first-served basis. If you can plan your stay during the week you'll have your choice of places to pitch your tent at SNP. On one balmy October weekend, the only available site I saw was roped off and set up with a bear trap. Take those warnings about using bear-proof food storage very seriously unless you want unwelcome visitors during the night.

There is no shortage of places to hike near the campground and the southern section of the park, in general. The Appalachian Trail loops around the southern end of the campground leading off from sites A-32 and A-8. In addition numerous trails are close to the campground.

One of the more popular side trails is the 1.3-mile Deadening Nature Trail loop. There are two rocky observation points which offer breathtaking views of the surrounding mountains and valleys. For a longer version of this hike, follow the Appalachian Trail north from the campground for 1.2 miles to create a 3.7-mile loop. Another hike that's well worth the effort is the 2.7-mile Loft Mountain Loop, which uses other trails as well as the AT to extend the Deadening Trail a bit. It will take you to a 3,290-foot perch on the side of Loft

Mountain for some equally awesome views. On a clear day you can see west to Massanutten Mountain.

To get there: From the Swift Run Gap Entrance Station at mile 65.7, drive south on the Skyline Drive to the campground entrance at mile 79.5.

KEY INFORMATION

Loft Mountain Campground
Shenandoah National Park
3655 U.S. Highway 211 East
Luray, VA 22835-9036

Operated by: National Park Service

Information: (540) 999-3500

Open: Mid-May through end of October

Individual sites: 219

Each site has: Picnic table and fire grill

Site assignment: Campers can choose from available sites

Registration: On arrival

Facilities: Camp store, coin-operated laundry and showers, restaurant, and flush toilets

Parking: At campsite

Fee: $14 in addition to $10 park entrance fee

Elevation: 3,400 feet

Restrictions:

Pets—Must be on leash shorter than six feet; clean up after pet; don't leave unattended

Fires—Use only camp stoves and designated fireplaces

Alcoholic beverages—Permitted

Vehicles—Up to 30 feet

Other—Do not carve, chop, or damage any live trees; wash dishes at campsite, not at restrooms, but gray water must be disposed of in service sinks at restrooms; quiet hours 10 p.m. to 6 a.m.; campsite capacity is six people, two tents, two vehicles per site

ELIZABETH FURNACE RECREATION AREA

Edinburg

The Elizabeth Furnace Recreation Area is located at the northern end of the 50-mile Massanutten Mountain, whose eastern and western ridges surround Fort Valley like the eye of a needle. Given its proximity to the northern Virginia–D.C. area, the campground and adjacent trail system get more than their fair share of use. The campground is located on VA Route 678 along the banks of Passage Creek. It's difficult to imagine it by looking at this narrow stream, but it was Passage Creek that carved out the area known as Fort Valley between the eastern and western ridges of Massanutten, thought to be a derivative of an Indian word for "basket." An early miner and counterfeiter named Powell is said to have been the first European settler in this small valley. He was so elusive that the earliest German settlers from the 1730s called it Powell's Fort Valley.

You'll find your access to this campground to be restricted after times of heavy rain when the creek overflows its banks. However, under average conditions, it provides a nice backdrop to this quiet campground with waters that are stocked with trout for fishermen. After passing the Volunteer Host site at the entrance into the campground, you'll find a large loop with some sites closer together than others, with 9–17 being the more private settings. The campground is flat and forms a large loop around a grassy central area. A

CAMPGROUND RATINGS

Beauty: ★★★
Site privacy: ★★★
Site spaciousness: ★★★
Quiet: ★★★
Security: ★★★
Cleanliness/upkeep: ★★★

An early miner and counterfeiter named Powell is said to have been the first European settler in this small valley.

WEST

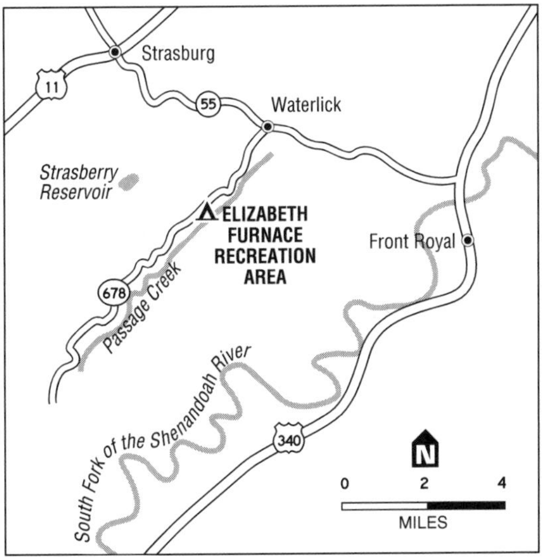

smaller loop near the campground entrance encompasses sites 24–30, but these are relatively close together. Water pumps and toilets are scattered about the campground.

Virginia's Shenandoah Valley figured heavily into the country's history, especially during the Civil War. Iron ore was an early resource that was mined, purified in furnaces such as here at Elizabeth, then shipped by boat on the South Fork of the Shenandoah River to the Hall Iron Works at Harper's Ferry, West Virginia. This iron was then used to make much of the munitions for the Confederacy. There are 14 similar furnaces in the Lee Ranger District. The 1830s log cabin at Elizabeth is open to the public on weekends as a forest service information center. Be sure to walk the Pig Iron (0.2-mile) and Charcoal (0.4-mile) Trails to learn more about this process.

Those looking for longer and more strenuous hikes can cross the road and climb on one or more of the area's well-blazed trails to the Buzzard Rock Overlook, Fort Valley Overlook, or Signal Knob. From its strategic location at the northern end of the Shenadoah Valley, called the Lower Valley based on the way the rivers flow through here, Signal Knob was an important Confederate lookout point to watch for the Union army in its attempt to enter and control the Shenadoah Valley. Although trail maintenance tends to be sorely lacking in most of the George Washington and Jefferson National Forests, Massanutten Mountain is a pleasant exception with its trails extremely well marked and clear of blow-downs thanks to the efforts of the Potomac

Appalachian Trail Club. Mountain biking is also a possibility on these trails, but riders should be prepared to yield the right-of-way to hikers who frequent the area, especially on weekends.

The yellow-blazed, 4.5-mile (point-to-point) Signal Knob Trail is a popular trail skirting the northern end of Massanutten. It offers some outstanding views including those from Buzzard Rock Overlook and Fort Valley Overlook. To avoid a nine-mile out-and-back hike, plan to return via the Massanutten Mountain West and Bear Wallow Trails. A particularly picturesque spot is Mudhole Gap through which Little Passage Creek passes between the Massanutten West Trail and the Little Sluice forest road. Mudhole's name obscures the lush beauty of this half-mile riparian area.

An especially fun time to visit the area is during the Elizabth Furnace Folkways Festival in September. Anglers will definitely want to bring their gear and do some fishing in the trout-stocked Passage Creek that runs through this Recreation Area along VA 678. Campers should note that although the campground is open year-round, the water is shut off from mid-October through the end of March.

To get there: From Strasburg, follow US 55 east for five miles to VA 616. Turn right onto VA 616 and drive less than a mile before turning right onto VA 678. Go 4 miles to the campground entrance on the left.

KEY INFORMATION

Elizabeth Furnace Recreation Area
Lee Ranger District
109 Molineau Road
Edinburg, VA 22824

Operated by: U.S. Forest Service

Information: (540) 984-4101

Open: Year-round

Individual sites: 32

Each site has: Fire ring and picnic table

Site assignment: At campground as available

Registration: In advance by phone, (800) 280-CAMP; or on arrival

Facilities: Water, hot showers, and flush toilets

Parking: At campsites

Fee: $11 per night from April through mid October; $7 per night the rest of the year

Elevation: 770 feet

Restrictions:

Pets—Should be on leash and attended

Fires—Use camp stove or fire ring

Alcoholic beverages—No restrictions on reasonable use

Vehicles—Up to 25 feet

Other—Do not damage live trees; quiet time 10 p.m. to 6 a.m.

LITTLE FORT RECREATION AREA

Edinburg

A story has been passed down that when things appeared their most bleak for the Colonial army during the Revolutionary War, Commander-in-Chief George Washington recalled his surveying days in western Virginia and considered retreat to a little-known valley, tucked within the "eye" of the needle-shaped Massanutten Mountain. However, Washington turned his army's luck around and his need for retreat to Fort Valley was obviated. Another story relates the mining and counterfeiting exploits of a man named Powell, thought to be one of the area's earliest settlers. He was said to be so good at hiding from the law that this came to be known as Powell's Fort Valley.

Little Fort Recreation Area lies on the western central flank along Fort Valley. While the "Recreation Area" part of this 10-site campground's name may be misleading, it remains a getaway for those with minimal need for amenities but desiring a secluded campground with access to the northern area of the George Washington and Jefferson National Forests and Virginia's spectacular Shenandoah Valley. Campers should be advised that Little Fort lies at the northern end of the Peters Mill Run ATV Trail, so quiet may be a variable commodity.

The campground loop offers better-than-average vegetation between the campsites. The sites are a short distance

CAMPGROUND RATINGS

Beauty: ★★★
Site privacy: ★★★
Site spaciousness: ★★★
Quiet: ★★★
Security: ★★
Cleanliness/upkeep: ★★

While the "Recreation Area" part of this 10-site campground's name may be misleading, it remains a getaway for those with minimal need for amenities.

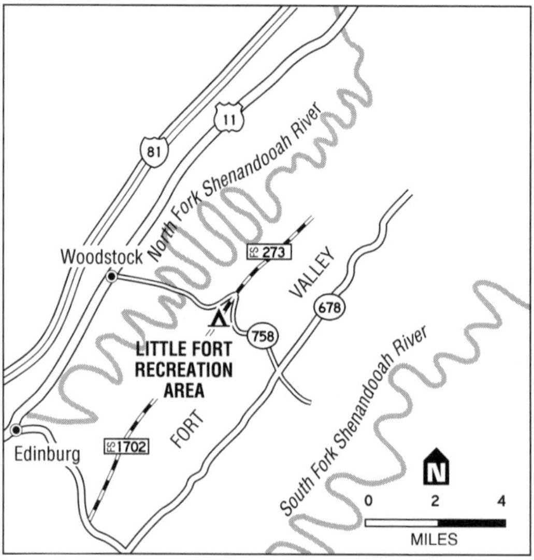

from their designated parking areas, which means that campers must carry their gear over from their cars. Once arrived, there are a some good options for trekking around. From the trailhead between sites 1 and 2, it's a steep one-mile hike along the Wagon Road Trail to the Woodstock Tower. The views across the Shenandoah Valley from this 40-foot tower are outstanding, but the most fascinating aspect is the view from on high of the Seven Bends of the Shenandoah River, which spread out some 1,200 feet below.

Little Fort is located in Woodstock Gap, just west of the town of Woodstock. This and other towns along VA 11, the old Valley Road, were the original turnpike towns and are worth a look-see for history and antique buffs. Road cyclists and motorcyclists alike will want to explore the quiet country roads of the Shenandoah Valley, as well as Fort Valley. You'll find that this small campground works best as a base from which to visit the neighboring countryside, rich with natural and historic treasures. Paddlers will find much to relish from this location between the North and South Forks of the famed Shenandoah River. The South Fork, which borders the eastern edge of Massanutten Mountain and the western edge of Shenandoah National Park, offers an ample number of canoe camps and public landings to provide entry to and exit from the Shenandoah. Be sure to pack a rod and reel for the abundant bass and panfish swimming beneath the surface.

Mountain bikers will find a number of forest roads and trails to ride. The previously mentioned 8-mile Peters Mill ORV Trail follows the top of the mountain south to Edinburg Gap, while FDR 273 goes north toward Elizabeth Furnace. Hikers are treated to an abundance of very well-blazed trails maintained by members of the Potomac Appalachian Trail Club.

One way to explore and get to know more about this 50-mile mountain range is by taking the Motor Mountaineering Tour of Massanutten Mountain that Forest Service personnel have laid out. A descriptive brochure offers points of interest from the tour's start at the Massanutten Visitors Center on VA 211 to Camp Roosevelt and onto Elizabeth Furnace at the northern end of Massanutten. Mountain bikers may want to pedal their way along this tour too.

To get there: From I-81, take Exit 283 into Woodstock. Turn onto VA 678 and then turn right onto VA 758. Follow this for 2.5 miles to the campground entrance on the left.

KEY INFORMATION

Little Fort Recreation Area
Lee Ranger District
109 Molineau Road
Edinburg, VA 22824

Operated by: U.S. Forest Service

Information: (540) 984-4101

Open: Year-round

Individual sites: 10

Each site has: Fire ring and picnic table

Site assignment: First come, first served

Registration: On arrival

Facilities: Vault toilet

Parking: Adjacent to sites

Fee: None

Elevation: 1,893 feet

Restrictions:

Pets—Must be on leash and attended

Fires—Use camp stove or fire ring

Alcoholic beverages—Permitted

Vehicles—None

Other—Do not damage live trees; quiet time 10 p.m. to 6 a.m.

CAMP ROOSEVELT RECREATION AREA

Edinburg

CAMPGROUND RATINGS

Beauty: ★★★
Site privacy: ★★★★
Site spaciousness: ★★★★
Quiet: ★★★
Security: ★★★
Cleanliness/upkeep: ★★★

You'd be hard-pressed to find quieter and larger campsites anywhere.

The future site for Camp Roosevelt saw history in the making on April 3, 1933 as the nation's first Civilian Conservation Corps volunteers arrived to create a camp to be dedicated a week later by President Franklin D. Roosevelt. The CCC, also known as the "army with shovels," was one aspect of Franklin's plan to deal with the Great Depression. The president did not make it to this first of some 1,500 CCC camps that would provide homes, training, and a sense of purpose for some 300,000 of America's out-of-work and work force. Despite the Great Depression's negative affects on the country, as a whole, the CCC's efforts created a heyday for the development of state and federal outdoor recreational facilities in Virginia.

Camp Roosevelt is located on Massanutten Mountain at the lower end of Fort Valley a short distance from the Massanutten Visitor Center location on US 211 and east of the town of Mount Jackson. After entering this recreation area at the intersection of FDR 274 and VA 675, you'll find the picnic area straight ahead and the campground to the left. The campground loop is arranged around a grassy central area where the bath house is located. The ten campsites are very spacious with ample vegetation and land between them. You'd be hard-pressed to find quieter and larger campsites anywhere. I don't believe I saw any in my travels throughout the

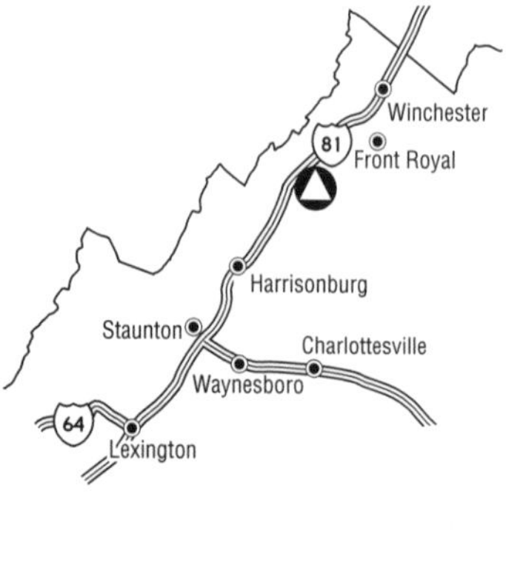

WEST

state. Adjacent to the campground is a picnic area where you'll find foundations from some of those early CCC buildings. A number of the CCC volunteers returned to this site and constructed the picnic pavillion "In honor of Leo Donovan, Captain US Army 1st Camp CO."

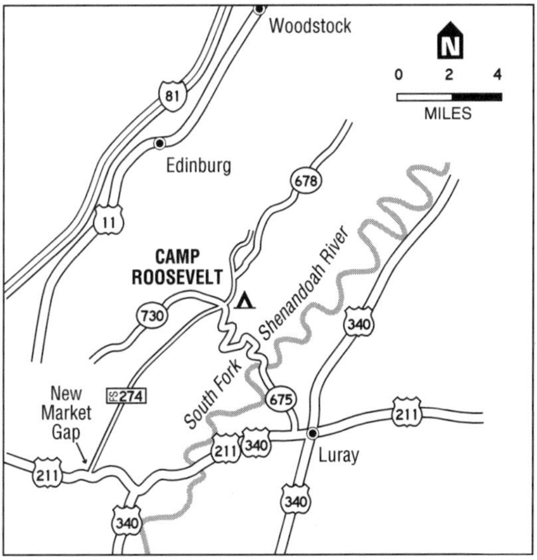

One way to explore and get to know more about this 50-mile mountain range is by taking the Motor Mountaineering tour of Massanutten Mountain that forest service personel have laid out. A descriptive brochure offers points of interest from the tour's start at the Massanutten Visitors Center on VA 211 to Camp Roosevelt and onto Elzabeth Furnace at the northern end of Massanutten. Mountain bikers may want to pedal their way along this tour.

Any number of well-blazed hiking trails run through this area for the beginner and the distance traveler alike. At the easier end of the spectrum are the paved 0.2-mile Discovery Way Trail and 0.5-mile Wildflower Trail, both of which are accessible from the Visitors Center. Moving north you'll find the 0.4-mile paved interpretive Massanutten Story, which offers signage to describe the vast geologic history of this mountain. At the end of the trail you'll enjoy some awesome views of neighboring Page County.

Mountain bikers and equestrians will find an extensive network of trails along Massanutten which can be pieced together with gravel forest service roads for a considerable number of routes. Especially nice is the 9-mile (point-to-point) Duncan Hollow Trail as well as the 2.1-mile Gap Creek and 2.8-mile Scothorn Gap Trails, which connect Duncan Hollow with Crisman Hollow, which has been carved out over time by Passage Creek. Anglers will enjoy going after their catch of stocked trout in Passage Creek.

In addition to exploring the beauty of the surrounding national forest, a campsite at Camp Roosevelt makes a great base from which to explore nearby attractions such as Luray and Shenandoah Caverns as well as the New Market Battlefield, the site of an 1864 Civil War battle in which 250 cadets from Virginia Military Institute fought.

To get there: From Luray, follow VA 675 for 9 miles to the campground entrance.

KEY INFORMATION

Camp Roosevelt Recreation Area
Lee Ranger District
109 Molineau Road
Edinburg, VA 22824

Operated by: U.S. Forest Service

Information: (540) 984-4101

Open: Beginning of May through end of September

Individual sites: 10

Each site has: Picnic table and cooking grill

Site assignment: First come, first served

Registration: Self-registration on site

Facilities: Water and flush toilets

Parking: At campsites and in picnic area

Fee: $8 per night

Elevation: 1,200 feet

Restrictions:

Pets—Must be on a leash no longer than six feet or under physical control at all times

Fires—Use camp stoves and fireplaces

Alcoholic beverages—No restriction on responsible use

Vehicles—No limit

Other—Fires only in designated fireplaces; campsites must be occupied the first night and not left unattended for any subsequent period thereafter; no destruction of live trees

HONE QUARRY RECREATION AREA

Bridgewater

The Hone Quarry Recreation Area lies at the foot of the Shenandoah Mountain on the western edge of the Shenandoah Valley and west of the city of Harrisonburg. It's located near the Briery Branch community along VA 257. Pull off the hard surface road onto FDR 62, and you'll arrive at the single loop containing the campground's ten sites on the left after passing the Hone Quarry picnic area. The picnic area is popular among Rockingham County residents, but with 23 grills and picnic tables you shouldn't have trouble finding a spot during the week. The campground is set among mature hemlocks with an understory of young evergreens to separate the various campsites. Given the vegetation and minimal number of sites, you're likely to attain ample privacy while staying here. Campers will find optimal seclusion during the week and outside of the busy summer months. However, the campground is a popular site for deer hunters in November, so plan accordingly. If you're willing to camp with minimal facilities, you can enjoy pitching your tent throughout the year.

The trout-stocked Hone Quarry Run borders the campground; but like many mountain run-offs, this benign stream can overflow its banks rather quickly after heavy rains and flood the low-lying campsites. So it's best to avoid this area after wet weather. On the other hand, the stream tends to dry up in the summer.

CAMPGROUND RATINGS

Beauty: ★★★
Site privacy: ★★★
Site spaciousness: ★★★
Quiet: ★★★
Security: ★★★
Cleanliness/upkeep: ★★★★

If you're willing to camp with minimal facilities, you can enjoy pitching your tent throughout the year.

WEST

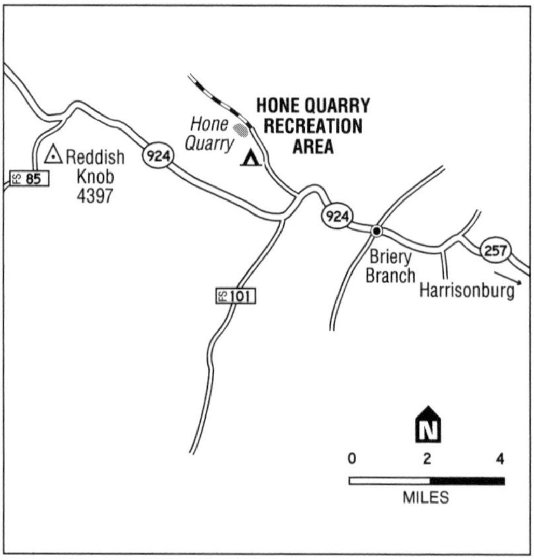

So somewhere in between you'll be lulled to sleep by its burble as it courses toward the North River.

Continuing past the campground on Forest Development Road 62, you'll arrive at the quarry itself, a very popular fishing destination with no swimming allowed. For an alternate fishing destination, Hearthstone Lake is just seven miles away on FDR 101 and Switzer Lake just north of here on US 33 in the shadow of High Knob. Of course, Hone Quarry Run as well as Briery Branch are options for those who enjoy their trout fishing from closer banks. Those looking to take a swim in the national forest will find the Todd Lake Recreation Area, some 12.5 miles south of Hone Quarry to be a very inviting destination.

For some of the more spectacular views into West Virginia and across the Shenandoah Valley, leave the campground and turn right onto VA 924. Keep climbing Shenandoah Mountain until you reach the crest of Reddish Knob. Don't be surprised to see some intrepid bicylists attempting the assault on Reddish Knob. You'll find parking as well as well an incredible panorama from this 4,397-foot perch.

This section of the national forest is very popular among Harrisonburg's large number of mountain bikers, and many of the more desirable trails and woods roads funnel down off of Shenandoah Mountain and converge on Hone Quarry. Mud Pond Gap, Slate Springs Trail, and California Ridge are but a few of the local, well-used trails within a short distance of the Hone Quarry campground.

This is a great area for hikers and equestrians; but just be prepared to share the trail whether you're on two legs, two wheels, or four legs.

FDR 62 becomes increasingly rocky as it climbs Shenadoah Mountain toward Flagpole Knob. Along the way the rough road ends where Mines Run Trail begins before merging into the Slate Springs Trails. If you're planning to do any exploring up here, you'd be wise to pick up a national forest map of the Dry River District. Hone Quarry is set among an incredible network of trails, and these inexpensive maps will give you an idea of the trails that surround your campsite. Undoubtedly you'll find, as I have over the years, that what's on the map and what's in the great beyond do not necessarily match up. And that can be the adventure or the danger of any outing in the backcountry.

To get there: From Harrisonburg, take US 42 south to Dayton. Turn right onto VA 257 and go 11 miles before turning right onto FDR 62 and the entrance to Hone Quarry.

KEY INFORMATION

Hone Quarry Recreation Area
Dry River Ranger District
112 North River Road
Bridgewater, VA 22812

Operated by: U.S. Forest Service

Information: (540) 828-2591

Individual sites: 10

Each site has: Fireplace grill, picnic table, and lantern pole

Site assignment: Camper can choose from available sites

Registration: On arrival

Facilities: Vault toilets and water

Parking: At campsite and picnic area

Fee: $5 per night

Elevation: 1,880 feet

Restrictions:

Pets—On leash only

Fires—In fire rings, stoves, or grills only

Alcoholic beverages—Prohibited

Vehicles—Up to 21 feet

Other—Do not carve, chop, or damage any live trees; keep noise at a reasonable level; non-gasoline-powered boats only allowed in quarry; quiet time 10 p.m. to 6 a.m.

NORTH RIVER CAMPGROUND

Bridgewater

The North River Campground is located near the southern tip of the George Washington and Jefferson National Forests' Dry River Ranger Ranger District along FDR 95B. You might want to think of this as an "uncampground" in that sites are not individually designated on the open grassy area, but campers are free to pitch a tent where they like, either on the inside or outside of the loop driveway. That explains why the number of sites given below is a rather vague "15–30." Since you are free to camp almost anywhere in the national forest unless otherwise designated, the question might arise as to why camp at North River Campground at all as opposed to merely pitching a tent somewhere across the road or through the woods.

In addition to having some degree of security with the presence of a campground host on-site, flat and open areas such as the North River Campground are pretty scarce in this wooded, mountainous area. If your tent is on the large side or you have several to pitch in proximity to each other, the relative spaciousness and flexibility here speak for themselves. While the unlimited size of sites might attract some RV campers, the lack of hook-ups and amenities will send most looking for a more "complete" campground. Those campers in search of good hiking trails and trout streams will find this an ideal site for a temporary respite.

CAMPGROUND RATINGS

Beauty: ★★★
Site privacy: ★★
Site spaciousness: ★★
Quiet: ★★★
Security: ★★
Cleanliness/upkeep: ★★★

Those campers in search of good hiking trails and trout streams will find this an ideal site for a temporary respite.

WEST

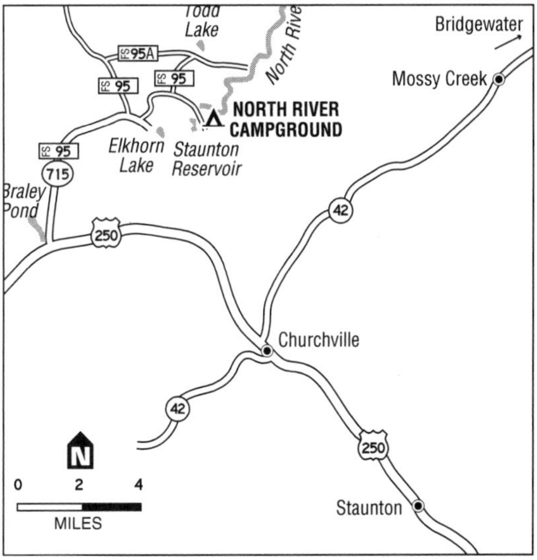

The four-mile (point-to-point) North River Gorge Trail is accessible through the metal gate at the back of the campground loop. This flat trail lies in a narrow valley between Trimble and Lookout Mountains crossing the North River a dozen times. North River can be very deceptive, sometimes appearing as a dried-up creek bed or a dangerous mountain stream depending on the season of the year and the amount of recent rainfall. However, during periods of moderate precipitation, the trail is a pleasant hike or mountain bike ride when the stream is fordable; and it was here that I saw, after many years in the outdoors, my first black bear in the woods. There are some nice pools for taking a dip should you be camping during the heat of the summer. However, you can expect this mountain runoff to stay pretty chilly throughout the year. The North River is a stocked stream and a great place for anglers to pit their skills against rainbow and brown trout. It flows into the Staunton Dam located just down FDR 95B from the campground. There you can also enjoy trout fishing, although boating and swimming are not allowed. Those looking to take a swim, have a picnic, or work on their tan on a sandy beach can drive (or pedal) a short distance along FDR 95 to the Todd Lake Recreation Area.

There is no shortage of places to hike in the national forest. A very popular, although fairly strenuous walk is the nearby 25.7-mile Wild Oak National Recreation loop Trail. This trail joins a number of mountain trails forming three shorter segments with three points of access from FDR 95, making it relatively easy to get on and off the trail after hiking a 10.2- or 5.2-mile stretch.

In addition to the aforementioned North River Gorge Trail, a more moderate hike in the immediate area is the four-mile Trimble Mountain loop Trail.

Mountain bikers will likewise find some enjoyable riding on nearby trails, forest development roads, or a combination of the two. One of my longtime favorites is a 14-mile loop that follows FDR 95 to Todd Lake, climbs along FDR 95A for several miles before careening downhill on FDR 95 to Elkhorn Lake. From there, it's a roller coaster of one- to two-mile ups and downs back to the North River Campground.

To get there: From Staunton, take US 250 17 miles to VA 715. Turn right onto VA 715 and continue past the point where the hard surface ends and the roads turns into FDR 95. Make the first right turn staying on FDR 95. Remain on FDR 95 to the intersection with FDR 95B straight ahead. Follow this road for a mile until you reach the campground on the left.

KEY INFORMATION

North River Campground
Dry River District of the George Washington and Jefferson National Forests
112 North River Road
Bridgewater, VA 22812

Operated by: U.S. Forest Service

Information: (540) 828-2591

Open: March 1–December 1

Individual sites: 15–30

Each site has: Fireplace grill and picnic table

Site assignment: Choose from available sites

Registration: On arrival

Facilities: Hand pump and vault toilet

Parking: At campsite

Fee: $5 per night

Elevation: 1,800 feet

Restrictions:

Pets—On leash and attended

Fires—Use camp stoves and grills

Alcoholic beverages—No restriction on responsible use

Vehicles—No limit

Other—Do not carve, chop, or damage any live trees; keep noise at a reasonable level; quiet time 10 p.m. to 6 a.m.

TODD LAKE RECREATION AREA

Bridgewater

Living just a half-hour's drive from Todd Lake over the course of my 20 years as a Shenandoah Valley resident, I confess to having spent more time at this recreation area taking a dip in the 7.5-acre lake after a rigorous mountain bike ride or a day-long family outing than as an overnight camper. However, whether you live a few hours or more away, you'll find that camping at Todd Lake will open a world of outdoor activity in this part of the George Washington and Jefferson National Forests. Public Affairs Specialist Nadine Pollack suggests that campers looking for optimal seclusion at this or any other national forest campground should plan their visit during mid-week or outside of the busy summer months.

This recreation area is located southwest of Harrisonburg. After a short ride through some of the Shenandoah Valley's more endearing back roads, you'll enter the Todd Lake Recreation Area from Forest Development Road 95, where the road turns from hard surface to the more typical gravel. The campground sits on a knoll to the left of the main road, and the day-use area is straight ahead just inside of the gated entrance. After a short downhill, you'll see the large parking area for the lake on the right. Continue past here for access to the recreation area's expansive wooded picnic area that ends at the edge of the lake. There's a roped-off sand beach

CAMPGROUND RATINGS

Beauty: ★★★★
Site privacy: ★★★
Site spaciousness: ★★★★★
Quiet: ★★★
Security: ★★★
Cleanliness/upkeep: ★★★★

Camping at Todd Lake will open a world of outdoor activity in this part of the George Washington and Jefferson National Forests.

WEST

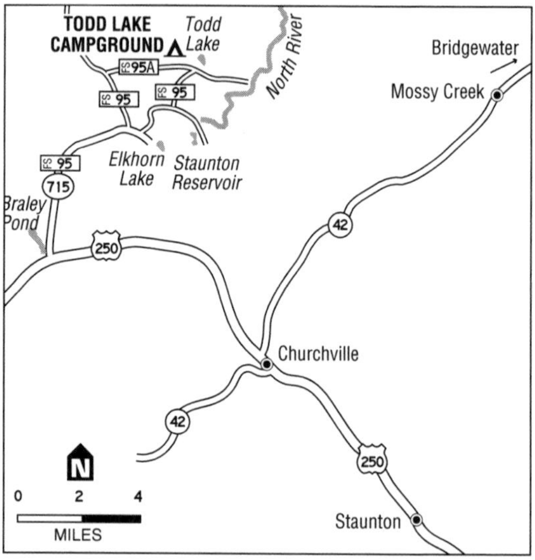

and swimming area, and the additional lake area is available for fishermen and non-motorized boats. However, boaters and anglers looking for a little more elbow room will drive a few miles to the larger Elkhorn Lake.

Half of Todd Lake's 20 campsites (1–4, 16–20) are spaced along the straight part of the camp road and the other half (5–15) along a loop at the end. The sites are as spacious as any that I've seen at campgrounds in the Old Dominion, and the feeling is enhanced by the dense second-growth oak and white pines that permeate the area. Sites 12–20 are also surrounded by profuse stands of mountain laurel. However, if that's not enough privacy, plan to visit during the week and head for site 12, which lies at the end of the campground loop with additional seclusion provided by high dirt berms. There are no bad sites at this campground.

Of course you'll want to spend some time on the sandy beach and swimming area at the lake. A foot trail located between sites three and four leads to the picnic area and lake a short walk away. Plan to enjoy a meal alfresco in the heavily wooded picnic area while enjoying the lake even though you've got cooking facilities back at the campsite.

Hiking opportunities abound in the George Washington and Jefferson National Forests, and the Todd Lake Area is no exception. A one-mile leg stretcher loops Todd Lake, while the four-mile Trimble Mountain Trail can be found on the opposite side of FDR 95 near the RV dump station. This loop follows the side of the mountain, but should not be too challenging for those with average fitness.

If you're looking for a real workout, drive on the hard-surface section of FDR 95 to reach the trailhead of the 25.6-mile Wild Oak National Recreation Trail. Don't let the distance or the terrain discourage you. Besides the trailhead, it intersects with forest roads in two other places, offering three point-to point day hikes. Segment A is 10.2 miles and climbs to the trail's highest point at 4,351 feet atop Little Bald Knob before descending to the North River (a creek, really) and the former site of a stockman's camp known as Camp Todd. Section B's 5.2 miles are said to be the most strenuous as the trail climbs slopes of up to 46 percent for a total of more than 1,700 feet before reaching FDR 96. Section C is 10.2 miles and traverses Hankey Mountain's relatively gentle slopes before crossing a steeper and rockier Lookout Mountain.

Area opportunities for mountain biking are unlimited if you use a combination of existing trails and forest service roads. I've long enjoyed the 14-mile Great Lakes Loop on gravel roads that pass Todd Lake. Start from Todd Lake and head uphill on FDR 95A and circle back around on FDR 95 along a series of challenging ascents and exhilarating descents while passing Elkhorn Lake and the Staunton Dam.

To get there: From Bridgewater, follow US 42 3 miles south to Mossy Creek. Continue on VA 747 where VA 42 bends sharply to the left. Take VA 731 for 1 mile before turning left onto VA 730. Go 3 miles and turn right onto VA 718. Follow this for a mile until it turns into FDR 95. Continue on FDR 95 for 2 miles to the entrance to Todd Lake.

KEY INFORMATION

Todd Lake Recreation Area
112 North River Road
Bridgewater, VA 22812

Operated by: U.S. Forest Service

Information: (540) 828-2591

Open: Memorial Day–Labor Day

Individual sites: 20

Each site has: Fire ring, picnic table, and lantern post

Site assignment: First come, first served; no reservations

Registration: Self-registration on site

Facilities: Hot showers and flush toilets

Parking: At campsite and day-use area at lake

Fee: $10 per night

Elevation: 2,000 feet

Restrictions:

Pets—On leash, attended, and under control at all times; not allowed at beach

Fires—Use fire rings, stoves, grills, and fireplaces

Alcoholic beverages—No restriction at campground; not allowed at beach

Vehicles—Up to 21 feet

Other—Campsite must be occupied the first night; not left unattended for a 24-hour period; 21-day maximum length of stay

SHERANDO LAKE RECREATION AREA

Lyndhurst

Living in the Shenandoah Valley for the past 20 years, I took the Sherando Lake Recreation Area somewhat for granted. Just a half-hour drive from my home, I enjoyed coming out for a day of swimming, fishing, canoeing, or mountain biking but infrequently spent the night. However, in the course of compiling information for this book, I saw Sherando Lake in a new light when compared to many other very beautiful campgrounds across Virginia. The name, Sherando, is thought to be a variant on "Shenandoah" which is widely translated to mean "daughter of the stars." And the campground here shines brightly as a possible destination for campers, not only because of its own offerings but also its potential as a base camp from which to explore this section of the George Washington and Jefferson National Forests and the Shenadoah Valley.

Nothing, in my mind, is as beautiful as a lake set against a mountainous background. This recreation area is tucked up against the side of the Blue Ridge Mountains on the eastern edge of the Shenandoah Valley. Turning off VA 664 you'll drive 2.5 miles on the hard-surface road that passes the beach and day-use area before passing campgrounds A, B, and C and finally ending at the Group Campground. Of the three, I think you'll find the White Oak Campground A, the first you'll come to, to be the most inviting. Situated on a hill-

CAMPGROUND RATINGS

Beauty: ★★★★★
Site privacy: ★★★★★
Site spaciousness: ★★★★★
Quiet: ★★★★
Security: ★★★★★
Cleanliness/upkeep: ★★★★

Sherando is thought to be a variant on "Shenandoah" which is widely translated to mean "daughter of the stars."

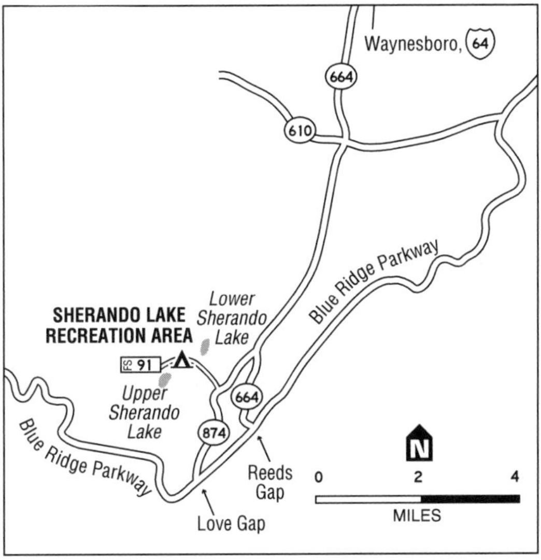

side of dense oak trees, the 34 sites along this loop are spacious and shady and offer more than ample privacy between you and your neighbors. The sites have been recently renovated, but you'll still find some of the original stonework from the park's construction by CCC workers in the 1930s. If you really want to admire their accomplishments here at Sherando, take a close look at the stone beachfront bathhouse and pavilion.

The Riverbend Campground, aka campground B, lies along the South River (actually a creek) that runs through this recreation area. It is flat, open, and the only loop that has hookups for RVs. A little farther down the road is the Meadow Loop, or campground C, whose 18 sites lacks hookups and are flat and open.

There are actually two lakes at Sherando with the upper lake near the end of the main park road designated for fishing. The lower lake has a beach for swimmers with a wading area clearly roped off. Stronger swimmers will want to practice their strokes on the way out to the island approximately a quarter mile from the beach. Anglers can cast their line anywhere along the shore away from the beach, although many choose to do so at the lower end of the lower lake by the dam. The lakeside trail will take you there as will a turnoff from the camp road one mile after the entrance station.

Hikers and mountain bikers will likewise find much to do while exploring trails that meander as well as those that climb up the surrounding mountains to the famed Blue Ridge Parkway. After passing site five on campground A loop, you'll notice the well-blazed Blue Loop Trail, which goes 0.5 mile to

Lookout Rock and connects with other trails for longer and more strenuous climbs, including a 4-mile ascent (one way) to Bald Mountain. The White Rock Gap Trail is a favorite among mountain bikers as a way to ascend and descend to and from the Blue Ridge Parkway. So whether you're looking for a little quiet time in the woods or a place from which to explore outdoor recreational pursuits, you're sure to find something enjoyable at Sherando Lake.

To get there: From I-64, take the exit for Sherando Lake located at the bottom of the western slope of Afton Mountain. Drive for 2 miles on VA 624 and then veer right at the bend onto VA 664. Follow this for 8 miles to the recreation entrance on the right.

KEY INFORMATION

Sherando Lake Recreation Area
Pedlar Ranger District
P.O. Box 10
Natural Bridge Station, VA 24579

Operated by: U.S. Forest Service

Information: (540) 291-2188

Open: April 1–end of October

Individual sites: 65

Each site has: Picnic table, fire grill, and lantern pole

Site assignment: Campers can choose from available sites

Registration: By phone or on arrival

Facilities: Water, flush toilets, hot showers, and drink machines

Parking: At campsites, picnic area, and lake

Fee: $15/night; $20/night with hookups

Elevation: 1,860 feet

Restrictions:

Pets—Must be on leash and attended at all times; not allowed on beach or in swimming areas

Fires—Confine to campstoves and designated grills; must be attended

Alcoholic beverages—Prohibited in beach area, parking lots, picnic areas; permitted at campsite

Vehicles—No limit at River Bend (Loop B) and Meadow Loop (Loop C) Campgrounds

Other—Quiet hours 10 p.m.–6 a.m.; length of stay is limited to 21 consecutive days; swimming and picnic areas close at dark; no cutting of live trees

NORTH CREEK CAMPGROUND

Buchanan

CAMPGROUND RATINGS

Beauty: ★★★★
Site privacy: ★★★★
Site spaciousness: ★★★
Quiet: ★★★
Security: ★★
Cleanliness/upkeep: ★★★

A no-frills area where you can pitch a tent in the shadow of towering hemlocks and even more towering mountain ridges.

While North Creek Campground may not be representative of all the campgrounds in this guide, in many ways it connotes (for me, anyhow) the essence of what *The Best in Tent Camping* is all about. It's a no-frills area where you can pitch a tent in the shadow of towering hemlocks and even more towering mountain ridges with few other campers around. It's several steps above backpacking in that you can drive to your site along a fast-moving trout stream and find a grill on which to cook your catch of the day or something from your cooler, with a picnic table on which to eat or just sit. But not everyone is looking for that kind of experience, nor is it readily accessible to most of you. And so the book contains a sampling of camping experiences with more amenities and ideally something for everybody.

North Creek Campground lies secluded at the foot of the Blue Ridge Mountains. As you'd expect, this campground is bordered by North Creek, a stocked trout stream that completely encircles this spartan 15-site facility en route to the James River located just west of here. All of these insular sites lie on a single gravel loop along the creek in an area of dense pine and hemlock trees with ample understory vegetation for privacy. Combined with the better than average size of the sites and separation from others, campers are likely to find ample seclusion here. Sites six and seven are designated as a

WEST

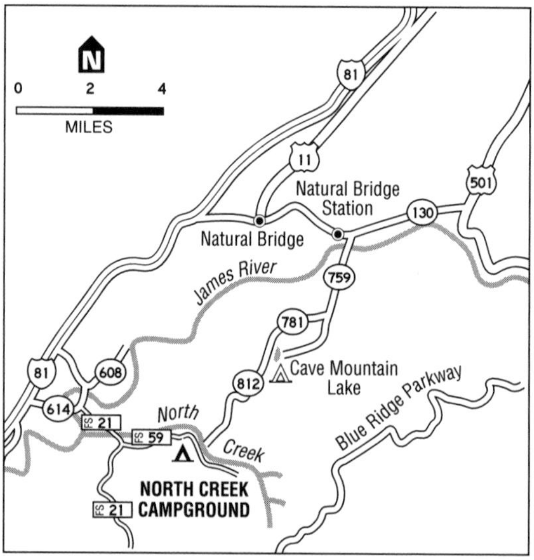

double site for larger parties, and all others are singles.

As beautiful as this setting is, visitors should keep in mind that mountain run-offs like North Creek are quite susceptible to flooding after heavy rains, so plan and respond accordingly. In addition, the campground and Forest Development Road 59 are situated in a narrow valley between neighboring ridges, so the possibility for flash flooding is increased and traces of past high water are readily apparent.

Activities at the North Creek Campground are geared toward this rich natural setting. Trout fishing from your tent site or somewhere downstream is an obvious choice for anyone with the inkling to test his or her angling abilities against stocked and native species. Fly fishermen will especially enjoy the special regulation area upstream from the campground where only artificial lures can be used. Check state regulations as to which specific licenses are required.

There are no shortage of hiking and mountain biking opportunities here in the George Washington and Jefferson National Forests. An especially scenic walk is the two-mile (point-to-point) moderate climb on the Apple Orchard Falls National Recreation Trail located at the end of FDR 59. The trail is very well maintained and graded as it follows North Creek up the Blue Ridge Mountains. After the falls, it's another mile to the famed Appalachian Trail, which stretches from Georgia to Maine. Mountain bikers will find even more opportunities to pedal through the area by tackling the 2.6-mile Whitetail loop Trail or heading out on neighboring forest development roads that loop across

Pine, Thomas, and Wildcat Mountains. Another option is to ride across Hoop Hole Gap to Cave Mountain Lake, take a swim, and pedal back to North Creek.

Whether you come here for outdoor challenges or quiet respite, you're sure to get your batteries recharged after a few days at North Creek.

To get there: From I-81, take exit 180 onto VA 614. Follow 614 for 3 miles before turning left onto FDR 59. Continue for 2.5 miles to North Creek Campground.

KEY INFORMATION

North Creek Campground
Glenwood Ranger District
P.O. Box 10
Natural Bridge Station, VA 24579

Operated by: U.S. Forest Service

Information: (540) 291-2188

Open: Year-round

Individual sites: 15

Each site has: Picnic table, fire ring, and lantern pole

Site assignment: First come, first served

Registration: Self-registration on site

Facilities: Vault toilet and water

Parking: At campsites only

Fee: $5 per night

Elevation: 1,200 feet

Restrictions:

Pets—Must be restrained and attended

Fires—Only in stoves, grills, and fire rings; fires must be attended

Alcoholic beverages—No restriction on responsible use

Vehicles—Up to 22 feet

Other—No cutting of live trees; quiet hours 10 p.m. to 6 a.m.; no fireworks, explosives, or firing of weapons

OTTER CREEK CAMPGROUND

Big Island

CAMPGROUND RATINGS

Beauty: ★★★
Site privacy: ★★★
Site spaciousness: ★★★
Quiet: ★★★
Security: ★★★
Cleanliness/upkeep: ★★★

Otter Creek runs near both the lowest point on the Blue Ridge Parkway as well as the Parkway's highest point in Virginia.

Otter Creek Campground lies near the lowest point (649 feet) on the Blue Ridge Parkway, whose 460 miles of two-lane blacktop are among the most spectacular in the country. Curiously, the highest point on the Virginia section of the parkway is approximately 15 miles south of here. This should give you an idea of the overall up-and-down nature of this road, although flat sections are also evident. The BRP begins numerically at milepost zero, located north of here at Afton Mountain, where Skyline Drive and BRP connect.

Otter Creek Campground is situated at mile 60.9, north of the James River and VA 501. The campground itself is located just behind the Otter Creek Restaurant and Gift Shop. After passing the entrance station and crossing Otter Creek, you'll find yourself at the center of a figure-eight road with Loop A for RVs on the left and Loop B for tent campers on the right. Loop B is further bisected by a road that incorporates sites 41–45. The level campground is wooded with mountain laurel, oaks, and pines, providing ample shade. The sites are well-spaced, although parking spots for some sites are adjacent and the accompanying sites also seemed relatively close together. If fishing for trout from your campsite or being lulled to sleep by the burble of Otter Creek is desirable, then you should plan to arrive during the week when you can get your choice from creekside sites 1–9.

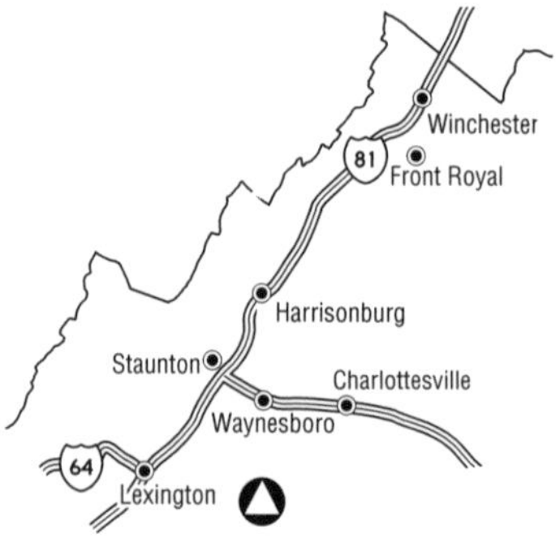

WEST

The 3.4-mile (one way) Otter Creek Trail is a nice, relatively easy walk that runs from the restaurant parking lot to the Otter Creek Visitor Center, located just south of the campground along the James River. It crosses the creek twice before intersecting with the 0.8-mile Otter Lake Trail, which in turn loops around this small body of water.

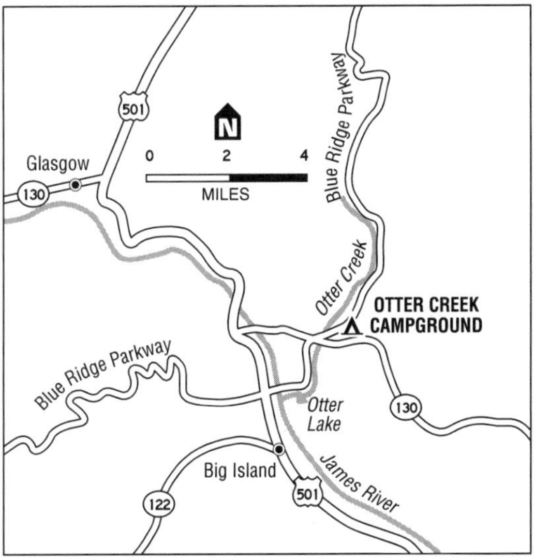

The Otter Creek Campground works well as a base camp from which to explore the area or as a stopover on your way north or south. Plan to pack your bicycle, if for no other reason than just to ride on the three-lane road that follows the undulations of the famed Blue Ridge Mountains. Paddling on the James, hiking on the Appalachian Trail that crosses US 501 just south of the campground, and mountain biking in the surrounding George Washington and Jefferson National Forests are all within a 15-minute drive. The Appalachian Trail and six others crisscross the 11,500-acre James River Face and adjoining Thunder Ridge Wilderness Areas just south of the James River. Nineteen miles of trails await mountain bikers and ORV riders at the South Pedlar ATV trail system, located a short distance west of the campground on US 501.

The James River follows the course of Virginia history, just like it has served as a major west-to-east transportation conduit since the first settlers followed it from the Chesapeake Bay to the site of Jamestown in 1607. The original plan was for the river to extend from Richmond to the Ohio River, but the James and Kanawha Canal only made it as far west as Buchanan, Virginia. Plan to cross the walkway over the James River and visit the rebuilt Lock No. 7 opposite the

Otter Creek Visitor Center. The Battery Creek lock is typical of the 90 locks that were constructed on the canal. This one in particular operated from 1851-1880, but the first section of the canal system was built at the falls in Richmond in 1795. Take a short walk on the Trail of Trees or plan a picnic lunch next to the Visitor Center along the banks of the James.

To get there: From Lynchburg, take US 501 west to the Blue Ridge Parkway at mile 63.8. Enter the parkway and drive north to the Otter Creek Restaurant and adjacent campground at mile 60.9.

KEY INFORMATION

Otter Creek Campground
Blue Ridge Parkway
200 BB&T Building
One Pack Square
Asheville, NC 28801

Operated by: National Park Service

Information: (828) 298-0398

Open: May 1–October 31 with water and toilets operating

Individual sites: 45

Each site has: Picnic table, fire ring, lantern pole

Site assignment: First come, first served

Registration: Self-registration on-site

Facilities: Restaurant, water, flush toilets

Parking: At campsites only

Fee: $8/night

Elevation: 777 feet

Restrictions:

Pets—On six-foot leash; owners must clean up after pets

Fires—Use campstoves and fireplaces; dead wood in the campground may be used

Alcoholic beverages—Permitted

Vehicles—Up to 30 feet

Other—Tents must be set up on tent pads; tents are not allowed on sites without tent pads; quiet time 10 p.m.–6 a.m.

PEAKS OF OTTER CAMPGROUND

Bedford

"The mountains of the Blue ridge, and of these the Peaks of Otter, are thought to be of a greater height, measured from their base, than any others in our country, and perhaps in North America," so said Thomas Jefferson in his only book, *Notes on the State of Virginia.* Given his expertise in architecture, law, politics, languages, and other fields, we'll have to forgive this bit of overstatement regarding the relative heights of Sharp Top and Flat Top, which stand at 3,875 feet and 4,001 feet, respectively. Given the manner in which they stand apart so graphically from their surroundings, it's easy to see how Charlottesville's favorite son could have embellished their stature a bit.

However, it's pretty difficult to overstate the beauty of the 470-mile Blue Ridge Parkway which stretches from Afton Mountain in Virginia to Cherokee, North Carolina. It's arguably one of the most beautiful roads in America; and the Peaks of Otter Campground, located at milepost 86, offers a tremendous place to pitch a tent for those passing through or intent on this as their final destination. Across the road is the picturesque Peaks of Otter Lodge, whose reflection is mirrored by Abbott Lake. You may want to sample the renowned bounty at the lodge should you tire of camp fare.

The campground's 144 sites are divided among three loops designated as A, B, and

CAMPGROUND RATINGS

Beauty: ★★★
Site privacy: ★★★
Site spaciousness: ★★★★
Quiet: ★★★★
Security: ★★★
Cleanliness/upkeep: ★★★★

Peaks of Otter offers a tremendous place to camp for those touring the Blue Ridge Parkway.

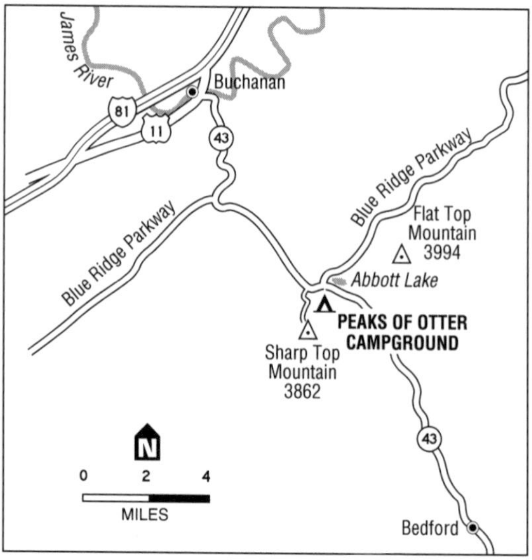

the trailer loop. If you've gotten fed up with those campgrounds that offer larger, more private, or more abundant sites for RV users, then you'll love the campground at the Peaks of Otter. There are only 46 sites in the trailer loop. There are no electrical or water hookups, the sites are similar in size to the tent sites, and the only concession seems to be access to a larger parking spot or a pull-through. How's that for egalitarian camping?

The campground is located in the woods on the flanks of Sharp Top. While some sites on Loop A all but border VA 43, which crosses the parkway here, the majority lie on the interior of the campground loop. You'll find the most private sites on the upper side of the loop road, most notably Sites A-19, 20, 23, 25, 29, 30, 35, 36, 37, 38, and 42. However, the concession to additional privacy is a 20–30-foot walk from your car to your tent up the slope of the mountain. The pattern is the same in Loop B with sites B-1, 2, 3, 4, 7, 8, 10, 13, 16, 20, 21, and 22 providing the most privacy with some additional aerobic exercise thrown in gratis. This may not be a big deal for some folks, but for others it's worth considering.

It's thought that indigenous people have passed through this area going back some 8,000 years. The first Europeans appeared by the mid-1700s, and an inn opened here in 1834. Many visitors to the Peaks of Otter plan their visit during the beginning of June when the wild rhododendron and mountain laurel are in bloom, but each season has its own characteristic beauty.

There are a number of area trails which the Park Service grades from easy to strenuous. The 1-mile loop around Abbott Lake located across US 43 from the campground falls into the former category while the 1.5-mile (one-way) hike up to the top of Sharp Top falls into the strenuous category. The views from the top are worth the effort. You'd be remiss, however, if you didn't also take the (one-way) 4.4-mile climb to the top of Flat Top. The Flat Top and Fallingwater Cascades Trail were designated as national recreation trails in 1982 and together offer both spectacular scenery from the series of falls and panoramic views from the top. You can also pick up several trails at the visitor center, located on the other side of the Blue Ridge Parkway from the campground. These include the 0.8-mile Elk Run Trail, 1.8-mile Johnson Farm Trail, and the 3.3-mile Harkening Hill Trail, all of which are loops. There a number of other trails that adjoin the Appalachian Trail and are accessible some five miles south of the peaks on the Blue Ridge Parkway.

To get there: Take the Blue Ridge Parkway to its intersection with VA 43 at milepost 86, and go 0.25 mile south on VA 43 to the campground entrance.

KEY INFORMATION

Peaks of Otter Campground
Blue Ridge Parkway
Route 2, Box 163
Bedford, VA 24523

Operated by: National Park Service

Information: (540) 586-4357

Open: May 1–October 31

Individual sites: 144

Each site has: Fire grill, picnic table, and lantern pole

Site assignment: First come, first served

Registration: On-site

Facilities: Water, camp store, and flush toilets

Parking: At campsites

Fee: $12 for two campers with additional $2 for every person over 18 years old

Elevation: 2,600 feet

Restrictions:

Pets—Must be restrained at all times

Fires—Camp stoves and grill only

Alcoholic beverages—Permitted

Vehicles—Up to 30 feet

Other—Quiet hours 10 p.m. to 6 a.m.

LAKE ROBERTSON

Lexington

The 581-acre Lake Robertson recreation area lies at the western edge of the Shenandoah Valley at the foot of North Mountain. Early Native Americans called this ridge Endless Mountain, and it's this image that you'll get looking up at it from the dam along the Lake Trail. However, an even better vantage point is from North Mountain itself. During your visit to Lake Robertson, try to schedule a ride up to the crest of this mountain for an incredible panorama of Lexington and Rockbridge looking west to the Blue Ridge Mountains.

It's a twisty but scenic route to Lake Robertson located near Collierstown, which is really an area more than a town. After turning off VA 770 onto the park's entrance road, you may be surprised to find playing fields and tennis, volleyball, and badminton courts as well as a swimming pool at this rural setting. These are, of course, in addition to the 31-acre fishing and boating (no gasoline motors allowed) lake. Rent a canoe or jon boat for a peaceful paddle or cast a line at the bass, walleye, and sunfish that call Lake Robertson home.

There are also a number of short trails from 0.25-mile to 1.75 miles that circle the lake and continue uphill behind the campground. Hikers and mountain bikers looking for a bit more challenge can link the various trails together or leave the park entirely and head for the wide-open spaces of the George Washington and

CAMPGROUND RATINGS

Beauty:	★★★★
Site privacy:	★★
Site spaciousness:	★★★
Quiet:	★★★
Security:	★★★★
Cleanliness/upkeep:	★★★★

Named for the father of evangelist Pat Roberston, this area is ripe with history and natural beauty.

WEST

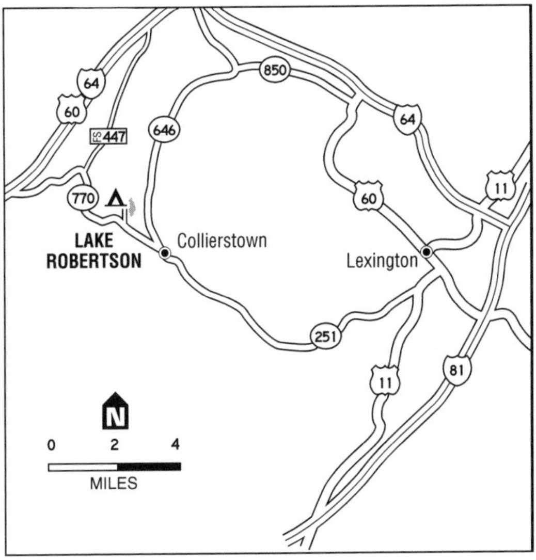

Jefferson National Forests which lie just west of here along North Mountain. The park's brochure includes a map showing the trails, which are also plainly marked as you traverse the wooded area west of the campground.

The campground is located behind the camp store and across the park's main drive from the lake. Situated in a grove of trees along a single loop, there is little undergrowth to offer privacy between sites but ample shade from spring through summer. The campground slopes gently uphill with plenty of space between sites, especially those around the volleyball court at the top of the hill. Sites 26–30 surround the grassy hilltop and are a little farther from the park's other activities, while sites 20, 21, 23, and 25 are nearby along the edge of the campground road. Tent campers should be sure to bring a ground cloth and mattress pad because many of the tent pads are gravel.

Those familiar with Virginia politics may recognize the name of former Sen. A. Willis Robertson, for whom this park is named. Most of us are better acquainted with the senator's prominent son, evangelist and politician Pat Robertson. As mentioned, this area is ripe with history and natural beauty. Surrounding Rockbridge County is named for Natural Bridge, one of the natural wonders of the world. Plan to take a picnic lunch to nearby Goshen Pass, an awesome scene where the Maury River has carved a path over time through the Allegheny Mountains. Lexington is the home of Washington and Lee University and the Virginia Military Institute. The town and county were the scene of important Civil War skirmishes.

You could use this campground as a base camp from which to explore the rich history and beauty of Rockbridge County and Lexington, located just ten miles away. However, you could just as easily park your car at Lake Robertson, pitch your tent, and savor the facilities that are provided here. Either way, you're sure to enjoy your stay.

To get there: From Lexington, follow US 11 for a mile to VA 251. Stay on VA 251 for 10 miles to VA 770. Turn left and drive for 2 miles to the park's entrance.

KEY INFORMATION

Lake A. Willis Robertson
106 Lake Robertson Drive
Lexington, VA 24450

Operated by: Rockbridge County Parks and Recreation

Information: (540) 463-4164

Open: April 1–December 1

Individual sites: 53

Each site has: Picnic table, electric/water hookups, and fire ring

Site assignment: First come, first served

Registration: By reservation or on arrival

Facilities: Camp store, pay telephone, laundry, drink machines, and modern bathhouse

Parking: At campsites

Fee: $15 per night for tent campers; $20 per night for trailers

Elevation: 1,540 feet

Restrictions:

Pets—Must be on leash, attended, and quiet at all times

Fires—Confine to camp stoves and fire rings

Alcoholic beverages—Prohibited

Vehicles—No limit

MORRIS HILL CAMPGROUND

Covington

The Morris Hill Campground is located just a short walk via the Morris Mill Trail (0.75-mile point-to-point) or the Fortney Branch Trail (1.3-mile point-to-point) from the southern end of Lake Moomaw. This 2,500-acre lake straddles the Alleghany-Bath County line with recreational facilities managed by two different national forest ranger districts, the Warm Springs District on the northern end and the James River District on the southern end.

It was formed by the construction of the Gathright Dam in 1981 and offers some of western Virginia's best trout fishing, both in the lake and the Jackson River, which flows from the dam. Some interesting tidbits about the lake are that its average depth is 80 feet, the shoreline is 43.5 miles, and its length is 12 miles. Boat length is restricted to 25 feet. It took two years to fill the lake. The northern end of Lake Moomaw is surrounded by the 13,428-acre Gathright Wildlife Management Area, one of the earliest tracts owned by Virginia's Department of Game and Inland Fisheries.

Anglers will find a number of fish, including largemouth bass, bluegill, crappie, and channel catfish. The boat landings at the southern end of the lake are Fortney Branch and Coles Point. Swimmers and sunbathers will find the sandy beach at the Coles Point Recreation Area to be a wonderful place to enjoy the southern end of

CAMPGROUND RATINGS

Beauty: ★★★
Site privacy: ★★★★
Site spaciousness: ★★★★
Quiet: ★★★
Security: ★★★
Cleanliness/upkeep: ★★★

The northern end of Lake Moomaw is surrounded by the 13,428-acre Gathright Wildlife Management Area.

WEST

the lake.

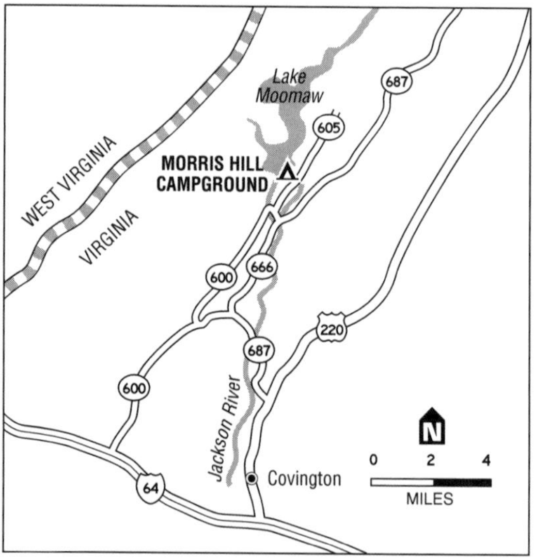

The Morris Hill Campground sits on a hilltop along VA 605 and is managed by the James River Ranger District. The single loop includes sites 1–38, which are available on a first come, first-served basis with sites 40–45 available through advance reservation. All of the sites are located in an area of mature hardwoods with enough low-growth vegetation to provide privacy between campsites. There is also ample space between campsites so that you won't feel that you're camping cheek to jowl. The center of the loop is a heavily wooded ravine, adding significantly to the feeling of being off in the forest.

In addition to the Fortney Branch and Morris Hill Trails, which are accessible from the campground, 5.3-mile (point-to-point) Oliver Mountain Trail is a steep climb offering some breathtaking views of neighboring peaks and the southern end of Lake Moomaw.

Just north up Lake Moomaw are 90 additional campsites at the Bolar Mountain Recreation Area managed by the Warm Springs Ranger District. While these hug the shoreline and offer some great views, they are laid out among three separate campgrounds and appear more conducive to RVs. I'd be remiss if I didn't mention these camping options so close by, but given the choice, I'd much prefer to pitch my touch in the relative seclusion of Morris Hill.

KEY INFORMATION

Morris Hill Campground
James River Ranger District
810-A Madison Avenue
Covington, VA 24426

Operated by: U.S. Forest Service

Information: (540) 962-2214

Open: April 30–November 1

Individual sites: 55

Each site has: Picnic table and fire ring

Site assignment: By reservation (887) 444-6777 or on arrival

Registration: Self-registration on site

Facilities: Flush toilets and hot showers

Parking: Only on campsite spur

Fee: $10 per night

Elevation: 2,000 feet

Restrictions:

Pets—Must be on leash and attended

Fires—Only in fire rings and camp stoves

Alcoholic beverages—May be consumed responsibly at campsite

Vehicles—Some sites will handle any size RV

Other—Quiet time 10 p.m. to 6 a.m.; campsite should not be left unattended for a 24-hour period

To get there: From I-64, take exit 16 and follow US 220 north for 4 miles. Turn left onto VA 687 and follow it for 3 miles. Turn left onto VA 641 and go a mile before turning right onto VA 666. Continue for 5 miles and then turn right onto VA 605. You'll find FDR 603, the entrance to the Morris Hill Campground, 2 miles ahead.

BUBBLING SPRINGS CAMPGROUND

Warm Springs

On my first visit to Bubbling Springs, I was amazed at how pristine the campground was. Admittedly, part of this assessment is based on its location in rural Bath County, and part is its lack of camping amenities that many on the KOA circuit take for granted. In the final hours of working on this book, I took a second visit out to Bubbling Springs for a combination of reasons. Would it still be a small, quiet campground that seems to attract little attention? It sure is!

If you're looking for a quiet, out of the way, no-frills place to pitch your tent and enjoy a pure camping experience, Bubbling Springs Campground, located on the western side of Mill Mountain, may just be the place. The area's five campsites are scattered a short distance from the central parking area, allowing plenty of separation from each other. All are set under a canopy of towering oaks and hemlocks, with thick patches of wild rhododendron at ground level. This campground is little-known outside of local outdoorsfolk and offers a quiet setting for those looking to enjoy the outdoors with few distractions.

If you look at a map of Virginia's Bath County, you'll quickly notice many place names end with the word "springs." Some were part of the extensive network of springs resorts in western Virginia that drew summer guests from all over the country. Those in Warm Springs are still in

CAMPGROUND RATINGS

Beauty: ★★★★
Site privacy: ★★★★★
Site spaciousness: ★★★★★
Quiet: ★★★★
Security: ★★
Cleanliness/upkeep: ★★

Lick Run flows along the perimeter of the campground, providing a perfect touch to this woodland setting.

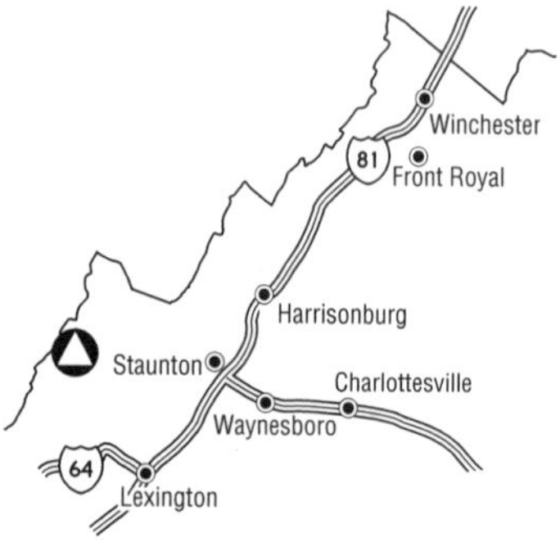

WEST

operation and open to the public. The men's facility located at the intersection of VA 39 and US 220 dates back to 1761 and was a popular stopover for many, including Thomas Jefferson.

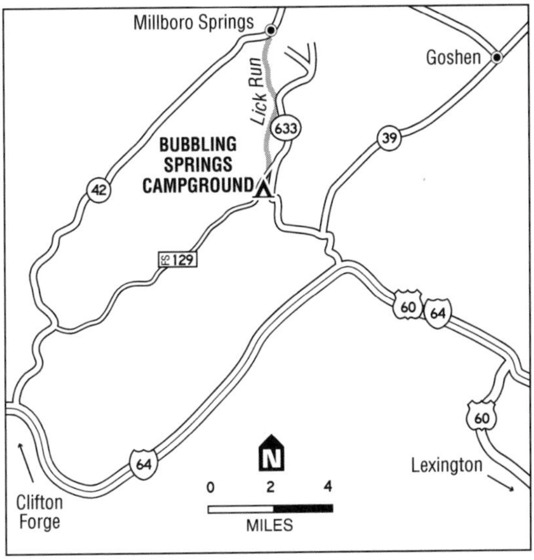

Springs are part of the karst—or limestone—topography that western Virginia is known for. These springs often lead to the development of caves, so it's no surprise the abundance of springs in rural Bath county is part of the state's longest cave network, the Butler-Sinking Creek system. Bob Gulden, a dedicated spelunker and cave mapper from Maryland, lists some 17 miles of passages for this system.

Even if you don't try the healing waters, there's little doubt that a weekend spent camping nearby has got to leave you better off than when you arrived. A well-worn but unmarked trail leads from behind the campground's SST (sweet-smellin' toilet) to the mossy groundwater surface from which Bubbling Spring emanates, providing the source for Lick Run along the edge of the campground. This narrow creek provides a perfect touch to this woodland setting, as well as a convenient spot to fish for trout. Pads Creek is another local stream that offers some challenges for those who like their streams narrow and their catch wary.

In addition to trout fishing, there are ample opportunities for other outdoor pursuits in this section of the George Washington and Jefferson National Forests. Hikers will enjoy the three-mile (one way) strenuous hike of Rough Mountain in the 9,300-acre Rough Mountain Wilderness located a short distance from Bubbling Springs Campground. There are numerous trails just west of the Cowpasture River and north of Douthat State Park. For that matter, you can relish the quiet at Bubbling Springs and still hike or bike the extensive trail system at Douthat.

The southeastern end of the 33,697-acre Goshen-Little North Mountain Wildlife Management Area is located just east of the Bubbling Springs Campground. Wildlife management areas are maintained by the Virginia Department of Game and Inland Fisheries but offer many opportunities for hikers, mountain bikers, and nature photographers. Be sure to check with DGIF to determine the presence or absence of game seasons at any given time, especially deer season in November. Order a copy of *A Guide to Wildlife Management Areas* from DGIF if you'd like to explore Goshen-Little North Mountain or other state WMAs. Pick up a Warm Springs Ranger District map if you plan to do some backwoods exploring or just to get a better idea of where this small campground lies in relation to Douthat State Park and other national forests.

I don't want to discourage anyone from camping here with the low evaluations for security and upkeep. This is a beautiful area that I thoroughly enjoyed, not a garbage dump with half-crazed criminals running around. In a minimally-developed campground such as Bubbling Springs, set in sparsely populated areas, you are a ways from civilization out here in the Alleghenies; day and overnight users may not clean up after themselves as they should.

To get there: From Lexington, take US 60 through town and turn right onto VA 633. Go 4.5 miles and turn left onto FDR 129 at the Bubbling Springs sign. The campground is 1 mile down the road on the left.

KEY INFORMATION

Bubbling Springs Campground
Warm Springs Ranger District
Route 2, Box 30
Hot Springs, VA 24445

Operated by: U.S. Forest Service

Information: (540) 839-2521

Open: Year-round

Individual sites: 5

Each site has: Picnic table and grill

Site assignment: First come, first served

Registration: On arrival

Facilities: Vault toilet and water

Parking: In central parking area

Fee: None

Elevation: 1,760 feet

Restrictions:

Pets—Must be on leash

Fires—Confine to camp stoves and grills provided

Alcoholic beverages—Responsible use at campsite is allowed

Vehicles—None, all sites are walk-in

Other—No cutting of live vegetation

DOUTHAT STATE PARK

Millboro

Douthat State Park's 4,493 acres are part of a 102,000-acre land grant dating back to 1795 which was given to Robert Douthat by Governor Robert Brooke. In 1936 it became one of Virginia's original six parks that comprised the state park system. This CCC-constructed getaway in far western Virginia lies in a valley between Beards and Middle Mountains, through which Wilson Creek and VA 629 run. The neighboring peaks reach heights of 3,000 feet while the lake is nestled at 1,146 feet.

The park's Depression-era beginnings led to its designation as a Registered National Historic Landmark. Great fishing in the 50-acre lake, rental cabins, and over 40 miles of hiking trails across the adjacent mountainsides are but a few of the attractions that draw large numbers of vacationers out to this rustic western Virginia setting. Stone walls, log pavillions, and wrought-iron attachments all speak to the CCC craftsmanship. The name of the park derives from early landowner, Robert Douthat, who received a large land grant here in 1795. Be sure to stop by the park's visitor center to get a better idea of its history. Another popular stop is the recently renovated Lakeview Restaurant and Country Store.

Douthat's 74 campsites are divided among Campgrounds A, B, and C. Tent campers without the need for hookups will head for Campground A, which is closest to

CAMPGROUND RATINGS

Beauty: ★★★★
Site privacy: ★★★
Site spaciousness: ★★★
Quiet: ★★★
Security: ★★★
Cleanliness/upkeep: ★★★★

This CCC-constructed getaway in far western Virginia lies in a valley between Beards and Middle Mountains.

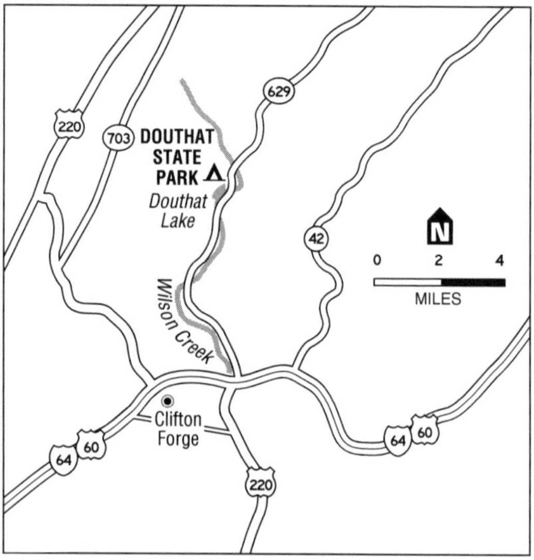

the lake. Although the sites are open with no wooded privacy barriers, the views of the lake and neighboring mountains are worth the compromise. Campground A is located in between B to the north and C to the south. Its 19 sites are accessible from VA 629 and tend to be the most popular because of the great views. Campground B is designated for group camping while Campground C is more oriented toward RV use, but the entire area lies under the shade of towering hemlocks with varying degrees of separation from each other. Campground C is south of the beach, located by the contact station. It is nicely wooded and private, especially those sites numbered in the twenties. Those looking to minimaly rough it at Douthat State Park try their best to rent one of the park's 30 cabins, 25 of which were constructed from logs by CCC workers.

Besides the overall rustic and natural setting, the park's main attraction is the 50-acre lake, which is regularly stocked with trout. Whether you fish from the shore, bring your own nongasoline-powered boat, or rent a canoe, paddleboat, hydrobike, or funyak (available from the beginning of April through Labor Day), you're sure to enjoy Douthat Lake. The 150-yard sandy beach offers a great place to cool off to lounge with the two-story concession building offering bathrooms, showers, and food available.

When all of Douthat's facilities are open from Memorial Day through Labor Day, there's no shortage of things to do here; so once you've pitched your tent, you can enjoy the area on foot, by bike, or by boat. There's a considerable degree of exploring that one can do in the neighboring national forest area, but Douthat State Park is a destination in and of itself. Depending on your interests, you'll probably find plenty to keep you busy on its almost 5,000 acres.

The park's literature lists two dozen trails suitable for hiking and mountain biking. These loop around on opposite sides of VA 629, which runs through the center of the park to create innumerable possibilites for tromping through the woods. A good a place as any to start is the 0.3-mile Buck Lick Interpretive Trail whose booklet describes much of the region's flora and fauna. The 4.5-mile Stony Run Trail is Douthat's longest, although, as stated, there are infinite possibilities for linking shorter trails into much longer, and more challenging, outings. Douthat is rapidly gaining a following among recreational and competitive mountain bike riders alike for the quality and challenge of the trails that traverse Middle Mountain, which rises to over 3,000 feet on the western side of the park. Competitive mountain bikers flock to the park in May for the Middle Mountain Momma bike race. Race Promoter Kyle Inman refers to the Douthat as "mountain bike Disneyland." 'Nuff said. Whatever your outdoor passion, the park's sheer beauty and opportunities for outdoor adventure make this a destination worth anyone's consideration.

To get there: From I-64, take Exit 27 onto VA 629. Follow this road for 7 miles to enter the park.

KEY INFORMATION

Douthat State Park
Route 1, Box 212
Millboro, VA 24460

Operated by: Virginia Department of Conservation and Recreation

Information: (540) 862-8100

Open: First weekend in March–December 1

Individual sites: 74

Each site has: Picnic table, lantern pole, and fire grill

Site assignment: Choose from available sites

Registration: By reservation, (800) 933-PARK; or on arrival

Facilities: Flush toilets, hot showers, and drink machine

Parking: One vehicle per campsite in addition to camping unit; additional vehicles must park in overflow parking area

Fee: $18 per night

Elevation: 1,367 feet

Restrictions:

Pets—On leash or in enclosed area; not allowed in swimming areas or toilet facilities

Fires—In fire rings, stoves, or grills only

Alcoholic beverages—Prohibited

Vehicles—None

Other—Swimming is allowed in the designated beach area only; length of stay no more than 14 days in a 30-day period

HIDDEN VALLEY CAMPGROUND

Hot Springs

CAMPGROUND RATINGS

Beauty: ★★★★
Site privacy: ★★★
Site spaciousness: ★★★
Quiet: ★★★
Security: ★★★
Cleanliness/upkeep: ★★★

The flood plain bordering the Jackson River, which meanders through Hidden Valley, has very old stories to tell about this area.

Tucked away in far western Virginia at the base of Back Creek Mountain, Hidden Valley richly deserves its name. Looking out across the pasture adjacent to this wooded campground, moviegoers might recognize Warwickton, the antebellum mansion that provided the primary setting for the movie *Sommersby*, starring Jodie Foster and Richard Gere. According to the movie's producers, "you could shoot 360 degrees and not know you were in the 20th century." Judge James Wood Warwick built the mansion in 1848, and it is considered one of the finest examples of Greek Revival architecture in western Virginia. It was placed on the National Register of Historic Places in 1973. The Forest Service acquired the building and its dependencies in 1965 in a state of disrepair. The roof was replaced to forestall any additional damage from the elements. However, it was in 1990 that a new life was given to this structure. Pam and Ron Stidham visited the area from their home in Ohio, and ultimately entered into an agreement—the first of its kind in Forest Service history—to refurbish Warwickton and operate it with the Forest Service as the Hidden Valley Bed and Breakfast under a long-term special use permit. The flood plain bordering the Jackson River, which meanders through Hidden Valley, has even older stories to tell about this area. Archeological excavations have

WEST

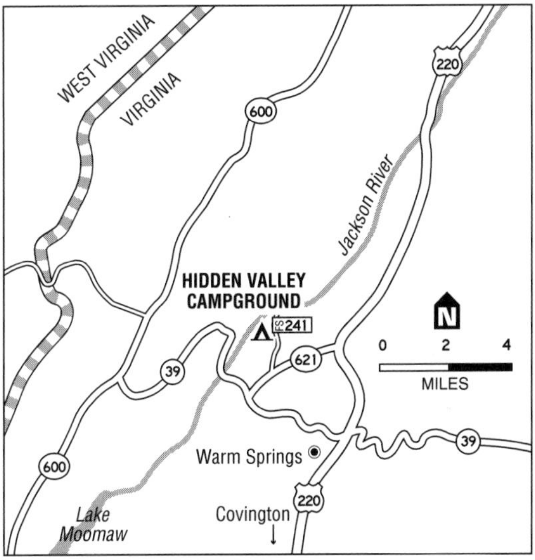

uncovered artifacts indicating the presence of Native Americans dating back as early as 6,500 B.C.

The Hidden Valley Campground is located in a wooded, level setting and offers a considerable amount of serenity, provided you plan your visit outside of the November deer season. Although Virginia's Department of Game and Inland Fisheries went to a year-round trout season several years back, there's still a contingent of anglers who make their way to this stretch of the Jackson River in early spring out of habit. However, most any other time of year, you're likely to arrive at the Hidden Valley Campground with your choice of campsites and few neighbors. The campground's 27 sites are well-shaded and set along a single loop. There is ample vegetation between the good-sized campsites to provide a considerable amount of privacy.

The Jackson River is an excellent trout stream and is accessible via the Hidden Valley Trail, which starts at the campground and follows the river for 6.2 miles—including several stream crossings sans bridges. This trail is also the start of a popular 12-mile mountain bike loop that circles back on FDR 241-2 past the mansion. Other trails include the 0.6-mile Lower Lost Woman Trail and the 1-mile Upper Lost Woman Trail, both accessible from the campground.

This is a beautiful part of Virginia, and although you can have a dandy time exploring Hidden Valley without getting back into your car, plan to allot some time for exploring the Warm Springs/Hot Springs area. No visit would be complete without a healthy dip into Warm Springs, located at the intersections of Routes 220 and 39. There are separate facilities for men and women, with the women's structure dating to 1836 and the men's to 1761, making it one of the oldest spas in the country. It's fairly well documented, however, that indigenous peoples frequented these springs as far back as some 9,000 years ago.

Western Virginia was once famous for its healing springs, and wealthy urbanites spent their summers visiting them to allow the waters to cure what ailed them—as well as to escape mosquito-borne diseases and partake in the social events held at these resorts. Hot Springs was initially developed by early settlers Thomas Bullet and brothers Thomas and Andrew Lewis in 1766. This majestic resort is one of the few still in operation and has hosted many notables over the years, including Thomas Jefferson, Robert E. Lee, and J. P. Morgan. Jefferson said of the springs in *Notes on the State of Virginia*, "They relieve rheumatisms. Other complaints also of very different natures have been removed or lessened by them. . . . These springs are very much resorted to in spite of a total want of accommodation for the sick. Their waters are strongest in the hottest months, which occasions their being visited in July and August principally."

To get there: From Warm Springs, follow US 39 west for 3 miles. Turn right onto VA 621 and continue for 2.75 miles to the entrance of Hidden Valley Campground.

KEY INFORMATION

Hidden Valley Campground
Warm Springs Ranger District
Route 2, Box 30
Hot Springs, VA 24445

Operated by: U.S. Forest Service

Information: (540) 839-2521

Open: Mid-March through end of November

Individual sites: 30

Each site has: Picnic table, fire grill, and lantern pole

Site assignment: First come, first served; no reservations

Registration: Self-registration on site

Facilities: Water and vault toilet

Parking: At campsite

Fee: $6 per night

Elevation: 1,800 feet

Restrictions:

Pets—On leash only and not allowed in swimming areas

Fires—In fire rings, stoves, or grills only

Alcoholic beverages—May be consumed responsibly at campsite

Vehicles—25-foot limit

Other—Do not carve, chop, or damage any live trees; keep noise at a reasonable level; length of stay no more than 14 days in 30-day period; quiet time 10 p.m. to 6 a.m.

LOCUST SPRINGS CAMPGROUND

Warm Springs

Locust Springs Recreation Area is tucked away in a corner of Virginia so remote that you'll have to enter West Virginia to reach it. This hidden corner of the Warm Springs District of the George Washington and Jefferson National Forests is not contiguous with the rest of the forest and was once part of West Virginia's Monongahela National Forest. You should know before making the trek that Locust Springs is not a campground per se but a picnic area where camping is permitted. What it lacks in amenities, however, it more than makes up in natural beauty and access to Virginia's most remote and biologically unique area.

The 9,900-acre Laurel Fork Special Management Area surrounding Locust Springs is part of the Potomac Highlands, and Laurel Fork itself feeds the Potomac River. In this biological niche you'll find 25 species of flora and fauna that exist nowhere else in the Old Dominion and are classified as rare by the Virginia Division of Natural Heritage. Due to elevations that reach 4,100 feet, you'll find a forest of birch, cherry, maple, red spruce, and beech that is more typical of northern climes. This is actually the eastern edge of a similar growth that covers thousands of acres in the adjoining Monongahela National Forest. You'll also find stands of mountain laurel that stretch to 40 feet in height. The wildlife population includes beavers,

CAMPGROUND RATINGS

Beauty: ★★★★
Site privacy: ★★
Site spaciousness: ★★★★
Quiet: ★★★
Security: ★★
Cleanliness/upkeep: ★★

In this biological niche, you'll find 25 species of flora and fauna that exist nowhere else in the Old Dominion.

WEST

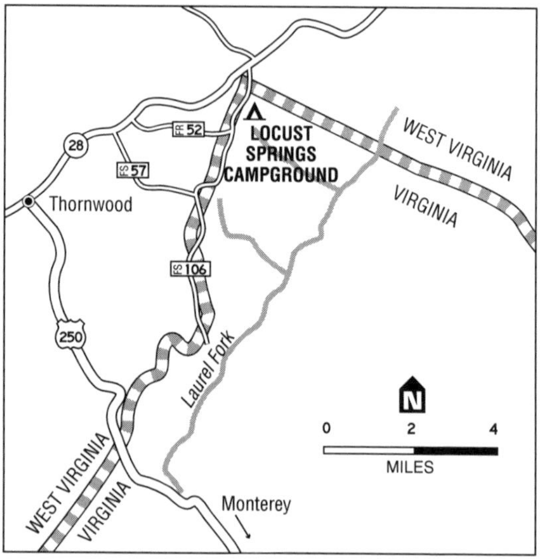

fishers, mink, muskrat, snowshoe hares, and flying squirrels. Pack your gear and fish for the brook trout that call these 7.5 miles of Laurel Fork and its tributaries home.

To reach this remote corner of the Old Dominion, you'll cross several mountain ranges in Virginia's Highland County. The region's ridges have given it the nickname "Little Switzerland," and it's often said that the county's population of sheep outnumbers that of people. You'll re-enter Virginia off of WV 28 onto FDR 106. Pull into the parking area at Locust Springs, and decide where on the grassy area ahead you want to pitch your tent. Peace and tranquility are an obvious function of how few people decide to camp here, as opposed to the typical factors of site and vegetation that would normally help to insure privacy. The general rule of thumb applies that staying here during the week is the best guarantee of solitude.

Given the location of this area, you'd be wise to bring everything with you that you'll need for a stay in the woods uninterrupted by off-site drives. Hiking and communing with nature on the more than 28 miles of trails are the primary activities at Laurel Fork. The three-mile Locust Spring Run Trail leaves the camping area next to the log lean-to and joins the Laurel Fork Trail. Given the extreme elevation at Laurel Fork, access to the Laurel Fork Trail can be severely limited by recent rainfall, snow runoff, and depth of the stream. The 6.5-mile Laurel Fork Trail runs along the stream of the same name through the middle of this lush preserve, with a number of other shorter trails, including Slabcamp Run (3 miles), Buck Run (3 miles), and Bearwallow

Run (2.7 miles) branching off and running uphill to FDR 106. These trails are the remnants of former tramlines that were used in the 1920s to remove timber from the Laurel Fork area. Prior to that time, red spruce was the dominant tree, but logging and a severe forest fire gave rise to more aggressive sweet birch, yellow birch, black cherry, and sugar maple. If you know your trees, you can still spot clumps of the original spruce.

To get there: From Staunton, take US 250 west for 45 miles to Monterey. Continue on US 250 for another 20 miles into West Virginia and turn right onto W VA 28. Proceed 6 miles and turn right onto FDR 106. Follow the signs a short distance from here to the Locust Springs Recreation Area.

KEY INFORMATION

Locust Springs Campground
Warm Springs Ranger District
Route 2, Box 30
Hot Springs, VA 24445

Operated by: U.S. Forest Service

Information: (540) 839-2521

Open: Year-round

Individual sites: 5

Each site has: Picnic table and grill

Site assignment: First come, first served

Registration: None

Facilities: Vault toilet and water

Parking: Adjacent to grassy picnic/camping area

Fee: None

Elevation: 3,720 feet

Restrictions:

Pets—Must be attended and kept on leash at all times

Fires—Use camp stove or grills

Alcoholic beverages—Responsible use is permitted

Vehicles—None

CAVE MOUNTAIN LAKE

Natural Bridge Station

There's nothing more splendid than a lake lying amid mountain peaks, and this is what you'll find at Cave Mountain Lake. The campground is a short walk in the woods away from the lake, a fact which has its pluses and minuses. While bereft of an immediate water view from your tent flap, this separation enables a certain amount of privacy from those who come for the day to swim in the seven-acre lake and feed at the adjoining picnic area.

After climbing and winding through a forest of pine, hemlock, and assorted hardwoods, the entrance road drops down into the wooded camping area. The sites are well spread out along a large loop and small spur with sites 36, 37, and 38 designated as walk-in sites that offer an even higher degree of privacy than the rest. However, the sites are spacious and the foliage of varying heights creates an ample degree of privacy. Tent pads consist of a fine gravel surface. Back Run courses its way through the campground before entering the lake. This placid stream is delightful when its level is moderate but can overflow its banks after especially heavy rains, so plan accordingly.

Located a short distance from Natural Bridge Caverns and Natural Bridge itself, the remnants of a cave disintegrated long ago, this area of the Shenandoah Valley is ripe with limestone deposits, sinkholes, and the accompanying caves. The 90-foot

CAMPGROUND RATINGS

Beauty: ★★★
Site privacy: ★★★★
Site spaciousness: ★★★★
Quiet: ★★★
Security: ★★★★
Cleanliness/upkeep: ★★★★★

Located a short distance from Natural Bridge Caverns and Natural Bridge itself, this area of the Shenandoah Valley is ripe with limestone deposits, sinkholes, and the accompanying caves.

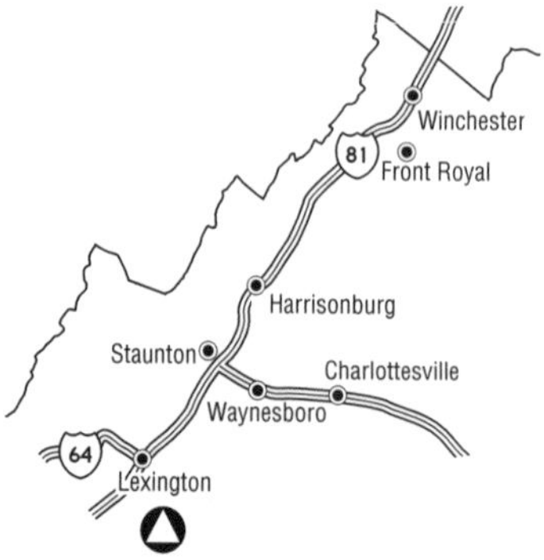

WEST

Natural Bridge is one of the natural wonders of the world. It stands 215 feet above the gorge carved out by Cedar Creek. First discovered and worshipped as a sacred site by the Monocan Indians, Thomas Jefferson bought it in 1774 for 20 shillings from King George III. Jefferson envisioned it as "undoubtedly one of the sublimest curiosities in nature" and planned to make it open for all the public to see. If you look hard enough, you can even see the initials of a young George Washington carved into the side.

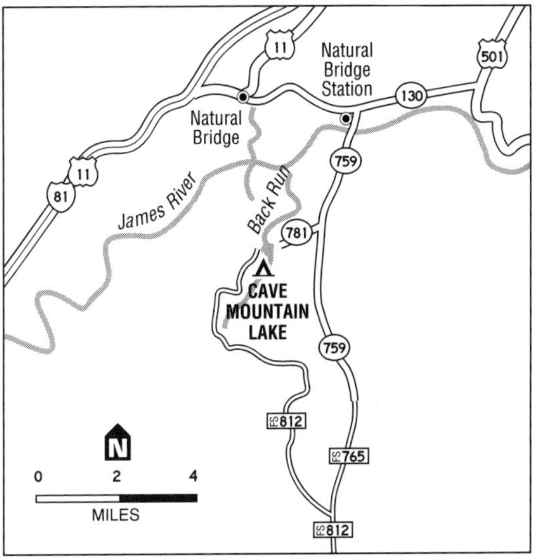

The other natural feature of the mountains bordering the Shenandoah Valley is the iron ore that the Confederacy depended on for munitions during the Civil War; and the nearby Glenwood Iron Furnance was one of over 100 in western Virginia that helped sustain the Southern cause as long as it did. CCC workers who were camped at what is now the Natural Bridge Learning Center constructed the lake, built the dam, planted pines and erected picnic structures at Cave Mountain Lake in the early 1930s. There's no shortage of natural and historic places to visit should you decide to use Cave Mountain Lake as a base camp from which to explore the area.

Both hikers and mountain bikers will enjoy the four-mile Wildcat Mountain Trail, which takes off from the upper end of the campground and gains some 1,500 feet before looping back. Adventurous mountain bikers can pair this trail with one or more area gravel forest development roads for an even longer outing. Those looking for a shorter walk should try the 0.5-mile Panther Knob Nature Trail. Additional trails, including the famed Appalchian Trail, can be found in the James River Face Wilderness just four miles from the campground.

In addition to the wide, sandy beach along the seven-acre lake, the day-use area includes a grassy area for tossing a ball around, bathhouse, and 41 picnic sites. The large log pavilion can be reserved by groups. All in all, Cave Mountain Lake's natural beauty and relative seclusion while offering access from Interstate 81 makes it a very worthwhile destination for those looking for solace.

To get there: From I-81, take exit 180 to Natural Bridge. Follow US 130 from Natural Bridge for 3 miles and turn right onto VA 759. Follow 759 for another 3 miles and turn right onto VA 781. Continue for another 1.5 miles to the entrance for Cave Mountain Lake Recreation Area.

KEY INFORMATION

Cave Mountain Lake
Glenwood Ranger District
P.O. Box 10
Natural Bridge Station, VA 24579

Operated by: U.S. Forest Service

Information: (540) 291-2188

Open: May 1–beginning of November

Individual sites: 42

Each site has: Picnic table, fire grill, and lantern pole

Site assignment: First come, first served

Registration: Self-registration on site

Facilities: Flush toilets, water, and hot showers

Parking: No more than two cars/site and confined to existing spurs and parking lots

Fee: $10 per night

Elevation: 1,200 feet

Restrictions:

Pets—Must be on 6-foot leash and attended

Fires—In fireplaces only

Alcoholic beverages—Prohibited

Vehicles—Up to 22 feet

Other—No destruction of live trees; quiet time 10 p.m.–6 a.m.

SOUTHWESTERN CAMPGROUNDS

CLAYTOR LAKE STATE PARK

Dublin

CAMPGROUND RATINGS

Beauty: ★★★
Site privacy: ★★★
Site spaciousness: ★★★
Quiet: ★★★
Security: ★★★
Cleanliness/upkeep: ★★★

The only Virginia state park with its own marina makes Claytor Lake a natural destination for boaters and fishermen.

Claytor Lake State Park lies on the 4,500-acre, 21-mile long Claytor Lake. The lake was formed in 1939 with the damming of the New River, just south of Radford, by the Appalachian Power Company. As an aside, the New River flows in a northerly direction and is thought to be the second oldest river in the world. The park came under the operation of Virginia's Division of State Parks in 1951. Its distinction as the only Virginia state park with its own marina makes it a natural destination for boaters and fishermen. The park offers bicycle and boat rentals as well as a fairly complete selection of supplies for water sports. As you might guess, motorboating and fishing on the lake are this park's greatest draws. Bass, catfish, muskie, and walleye are the favorite catch of anglers. In addition, the 450-foot sandy beach and six group picnic shelters provide activities for landlubbers. Those without boats will find a number of excellent coves along the shoreline from which to fish. However, the four campground loops offer the option of sleeping out under the trees whether or not you've towed your boat and brought your rod and reel.

After passing the contact station, you'll see the campground entrance on the right. Enter here and signs will direct you to loops A and B on the right and loops C and D on the left. Park personnel have recently refurbished sites in loops A, B, and C. The sites

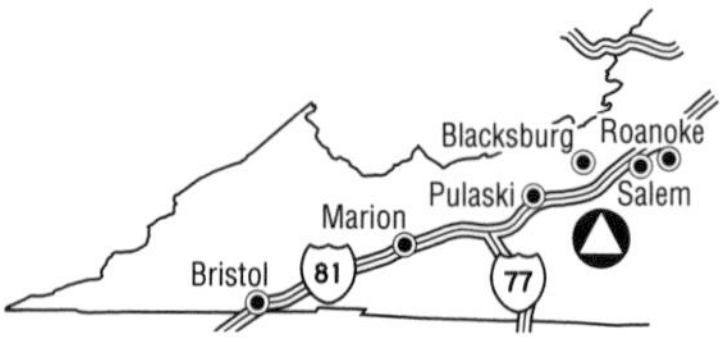

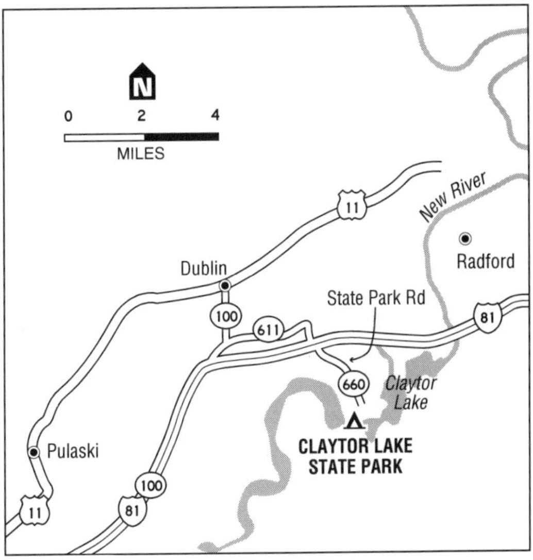

are very large, with a fine gravel surface bounded by landscape timbers, but they offer no electrical hookups at this time. Tent campers should be sure to bring a ground cloth and some sort of mattress pad. The canopy of mature pines and hardwoods creates considerable shade for loops A, B, and C, although there is minimal understory for privacy between sites. In this respect, you might want to look at sites A9–A27, which are flat but laid out on a hillside.

Loop D has a much different feel than A, B, and C. In addition to being positioned along a flat open area, it's the only one without delineated tent pads. So you have the option to pitch your tent on terra firma, either in the open or among groves of pine trees. Loop D sites are laid out along three lines, but D30–D36 seemed to be the most private, with the dirt access road in front and a buffer of pine trees behind them. Despite its appearance as somewhat more conducive to tent camping than the other loops, it's also the only one with electrical hookups. Go figure.

The park has six picnic shelters that are available for rent, and four miles of trails for an easy walk through the woods. You can pick up the 1.6-mile Claytor Lake Trail across from site C4, while the 0.6-mile Shady Ridge Trail is accessible from the picnic area. Mountain bikers may want to use Claytor Lake State Park to ride on the 57-mile New River Trail, part of which runs along Claytor Lake.

Be sure to stop by the Historic Howe House, built in the late 1870s by Haven B. Howe. Besides being a Civil War veteran, Virginia legislator, and talented woodworker, Howe was an early environmentalist who worked to end pollution of the New River by iron ore smelting plants. The building, made with brick kiln-dried on the property and timber felled from the surrounding woods, now houses the park's visitor center and administrative offices. It contains hands-on exhibits which focus on lake ecology and fish life as well as the park's Discovery Center, which offers summer environmental education programs. Check at the visitor center to see which guided interpretive programs are going on during your stay at the park.

To get there: From I-81, take exit 101 and drive 2 miles on VA 660 to the park's entrance.

KEY INFORMATION

Claytor Lake State Park
4400 State Park Road
Dublin, VA 24084

Operated by: Virginia Department of Conservation and Recreation

Information: (540) 674-5492

Open: April 1–December 1

Individual sites: 117

Each site has: Picnic table, fire grill, and lantern pole(s)

Site assignment: By reservation, (800) 933-PARK; and first come, first served

Registration: On-site

Facilities: Flush toilets and hot showers; pay telephone and drink machines at marina

Parking: Ample parking at campsites

Fee: $14 per night; $18 with hookups

Elevation: 1,900 feet

Restrictions:

Pets—Must be on six-foot leash and attended

Fires—Contained to camp stoves and fire rings

Alcoholic beverages—Prohibited

Vehicles—Up to 35 feet

Other—Swimming only in designated areas; no cutting of trees

GRAYSON HIGHLANDS STATE PARK

Mouth of Wilson

CAMPGROUND RATINGS

Beauty: ★★★★
Site privacy: ★★★
Site spaciousness: ★★★
Quiet: ★★★
Security: ★★★
Cleanliness/upkeep: ★★★★

The overall feeling is that you're clinging to the roof of the Old Dominion.

With elevations up to 5,089 feet, Grayson Highlands is the loftiest state park in Virginia. It was originally known as Mount Rogers State Park when it became part of the state system in 1965. As you enter the park from US 58 at 3,698 feet and ascend to the visitor center at 4,953 feet, you get the feeling that you're climbing into heaven. And for many campers, that's exactly where you're headed. From the Pinnacles, Grayson Highlands' highest point, you'll find breathtaking views of surrounding mountains, including Mount Rogers (5,729 feet), the tallest peak in Virginia. The overall feeling is not that you're on an isolated elevation but more like you're clinging to the roof of the Old Dominion. The mountains in this region are thought to have been volcanic once, and their rhyolite is less susceptible to weathering than other forms of Virginia rock and minerals.

After passing the contact station, you'll notice the park's office on the left. It's another 2.5 miles to the turnoff for the campground by the overnight parking area for backpackers. Grayson Highlands also has the distinction of being one of two Virginia State Parks through which the 2,160-mile Appalachian Trail passes on its way between Maine and Georgia. Thus, it's a popular spot for through-hikers as well as those looking to enhance their hiking experience with some AT mileage.

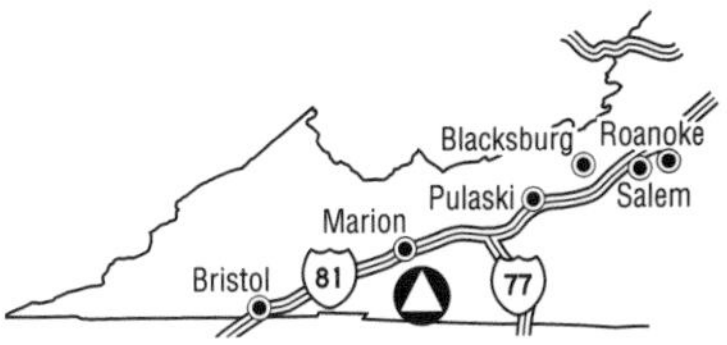

SOUTHWEST

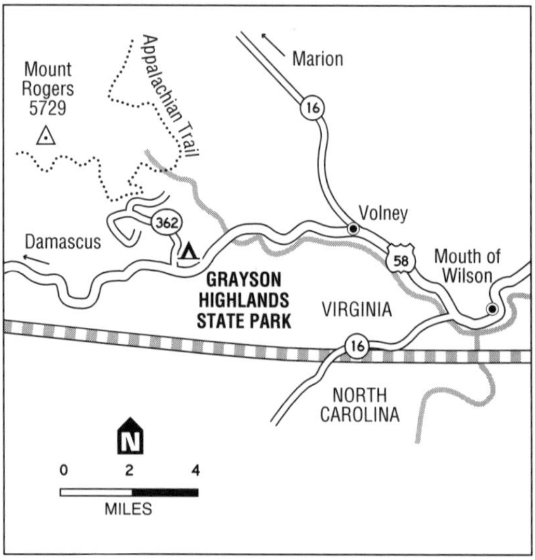

The campground is off by itself, and your first glimpse will be of those sites clustered around a grassy bald knoll. The campground's 75 sites are positioned along two interlocking loops. You'll find considerable differences in privacy and exposure among the various sites. Once you get past the first bathhouse, you'll find that the woods become more invasive. However, on top of elevations such as this, trees have a tough time getting much height. If you have a choice, it's definitely worth a drive or two around to pick out your favorite, especially if you plan to spend a few days here. Sites 49–59 at the rear of the loop under the shade of overhanging hardwoods looked particularly appealing to me. All sites have a gravel base, so it's highly recommended that you pack a ground cloth and sleeping pad.

Its location on the southern edge of the Mount Rogers National Recreation Area and the Little Wilson Creek Wilderness Area helps attract a considerable number of visitors every year to this 4,935-acre palace among the clouds. Equestrian facilities as well as hiking and mountain bike trails bring together a cross section of outdoor enthusiasts to enjoy this alpine environment. Backcountry fly fishermen will enjoy casting a line onto Cabin and Wilson Creeks, which are special regulation areas. Contact park officials for specific rules and license requirements. Depending on your particular interests, you'll want to pick up a copy of the park's *Mountain Bike Trail Guide* or *Horse Trail Guide.*

The visitor center is located near the summit of Haw Orchard Mountain and trailheads for the Twin Pinnacles and Listening Rock Trails. Inside you'll find fascinating exhibits of the area's geology and history of the rough life that European settlers led here, including one on the how-tos of whiskey making. The Mountain Crafts Shop, located in this stone and timber building, will give you the opportunity to purchase gifts made by local artisans of the Rooftop of Virginia Community Action Program.

You'll definitely want to take the half-hour walk up the Big Pinnacle Trail, which offers incredible views of Virginia's two tallest mountains, Mount Rogers and White Top (5,344 feet) in addition to the surrounding "lowlands" of Virginia, North Carolina, and Tennessee. There are other trails in the park that can be strung together for longer and more varied hikes. You can reach Mount Rogers by taking the Rhododendron Trail from the Massie Gap parking area to the Appalachian Trail and continuing on the AT for a four-mile (one-way) hike. The hike is moderately challenging, but don't go expecting to find tremendous views from this lofty point. Mount Rogers is capped by spruce trees and offers no views at all.

When planning your trip to Grayson Highlands State Park, you might want to avoid the dates for one of the many festivals that take place here from March through October. However, keep in mind that the weather can change rapidly, so be sure to pack for extremes of temperature. One balmy Easter Sunday I was hiking around the park in shorts and a T-shirt only to be snowed on that evening.

To get there: From I-81, take exit 45 at Marion and drive 33 miles south on US 16. Turn right onto US 58 in the community of Volney and continue 8 miles to the park's entrance.

KEY INFORMATION

Grayson Highlands State Park
829 Grayson Highland Lane
Mouth of Wilson, VA 24363

Operated by: Virginia Department of Conservation and Recreation

Information: (540) 579-7092

Open: First weekend in March–December 1

Individual sites: 75

Each site has: Picnic table, fire ring, and lantern pole

Site assignment: First come, first served

Registration: On arrival or by phone, (800) 933-PARK

Facilities: Laundry, camp store, pay telephone, and hot showers

Parking: At campsite

Fee: $14 per night; $18 with electric hookup

Elevation: 4,000 feet

Restrictions:

Pets—Not allowed in public facilities

Fires—In grills, stoves, and fire rings

Alcoholic beverages—Public use is prohibited

Vehicles—Up to 40 feet

Other—Length of stay no more than 14 days in a 30-day period

HUNGRY MOTHER STATE PARK

Marion

Hungry Mother State Park is one of the original six parks that formed the nucleus of Virginia's state system in 1936. The legend behind this park's name is every bit as colorful as the foliage that wraps around this setting in the fall. Back in Virginia's past when relations between settlers and local Indians was at an ebb, it's said that a party of Native American warriors destroyed several settlements south of what is now the park on the New River. Molly Marley and her child escaped the attacks but were taken captive. They were eventually able to escape, subsisting on wild berries as they made their way through the wilderness. Molly finally collapsed while her child continued by following a creek. When the child found help, its only words were, "hungry, mother." The search party followed the creek and found Molly dead. They named the mountain, at whose base they found her, Molly's Knob, and the creek became known as Hungry Mother Creek. With the formation of the park in the 1930s, the creek was dammed to form Hungry Mother Lake.

The park is located four miles from Marion on VA 16, which passes through the park boundaries. It contains 43 sites distributed over three campgrounds. Campground A is located alongside VA 16 and adjacent to the park's horse stables. This campground sits on a small field with no vegetation between sites and offers little in

CAMPGROUND RATINGS

Beauty: ★★★★
Site privacy: ★★★★
Site spaciousness: ★★★★
Quiet: ★★★★
Security: ★★★
Cleanliness/upkeep: ★★★★

Swimming, boating, and fishing for northern pike—reputedly the best in the state—are just a few of the possibilities here.

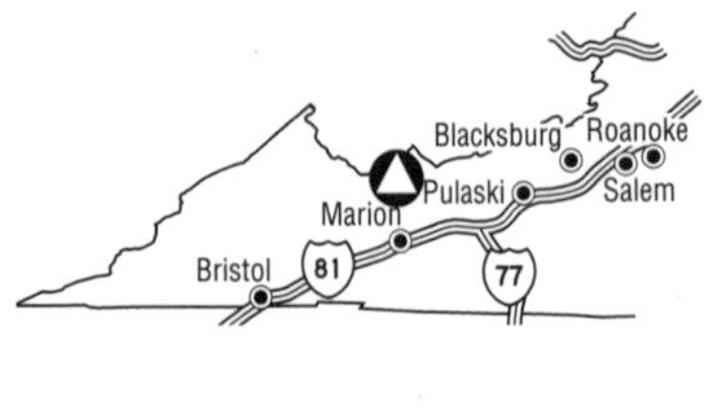

SOUTHWEST

the way of atmosphere, privacy, or seclusion. Campground B is located across VA 348 and is very much RV-oriented. Its 21 sites have electric and water hookups and are situated close to each other along a maze of hard surface roads.

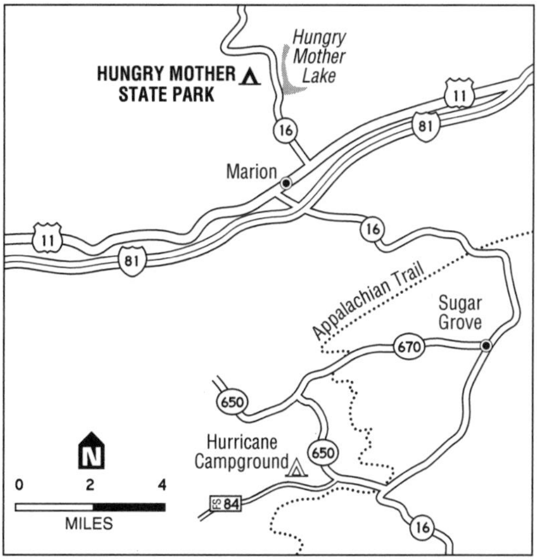

This leaves campground C, situated on a neighboring, wooded hilltop. Park designers utilized this uneven surface by erecting wooden decking for tent pads for most of the sites along this single loop. In my travels visiting Virginia's campgrounds, Hungry Mother was the only place where I had the occasion to sleep on a boardwalk surface. I'm accustomed to sleeping on a firm surface, so I appreciated its evenness; however, you may not. These sites are interspersed among a forest of oaks and immature pines with some vegetation between them. However, the positioning of the "tent decks" in terms of location and elevation offer the camper a modicum of privacy at campground C. Sites 4 and 8 offer gravel tent pads rather than decking, and sites 8 through 11 offer the greatest distance between campers.

Swimming, boating, and fishing for northern pike—reputed to be the best in the state—in the 108-acre Hungry Mother Lake are but a few of the activities at the park. This 2,215-acre getaway offers more than 12 miles of trails for hiking and biking as well as horseback riding for those renting horses from the park's concessionaire from Memorial Day through Labor Day when most of the facilities are open. This is the only Virginia state park with guided horseback trails. Bicycles are only allowed on the 2.7-mile Lake Trail and 0.9-mile Raider's Run Trail.

The third week of July, escape the heat when the Hungry Mother Arts and Crafts Festival takes place. However, any number of other programs are offered, including the Wee Naturalist outings for preschoolers, night hikes, and Music in the Park on Saturday nights at the amphitheater. There are also programs of interest on Sunday afternoons and Friday evenings whose topics have included building bat houses, Appalachian toys, and bird feeders with special guests on hand for storytelling, stargazing, and square dancing. A newly initiated program for the summer of 1999 was a weekly Junior Naturalist series for 6- to 12-year-olds. In short, there is plenty going on at Hungry Mother State Park for the entire family.

To get ther: From I-81, take exit 47 heading toward Marion. Turn right in Marion onto US 16 and continue for 4 miles to the park's entrance.

KEY INFORMATION

Hungry Mother State Park
2854 Park Boulevard
Marion, VA 24354

Operated by: Virginia Department of Conservation and Recreation

Information: (540) 781-7400

Open: First weekend in March–December 1

Individual sites: 43

Each site has: Picnic table and fire grill

Site assignment: First come, first served

Registration: (800) 933-PARK or on arrival

Facilities: Restaurant, flush toilets, and showers

Parking: One vehicle in addition to camping unit at site

Fee: $14/$18 with water and electricity

Elevation: 2,400 feet

Restrictions:

Pets—Must be on six-foot leash and attended

Fires—Use camp stove or fire ring

Alcoholic beverages—Public use or display is prohibited

Vehicles—Up to 30 feet

Other—Swimming only in designated areas; no cutting of trees; gasoline motors not allowed on lake

THE PINES CAMPGROUND

New Castle

The Pines Campground lies on the northeast edge of the 5,700-acre Barbours Creek Wilderness, at the foot of Potts Mountain, in the New Castle Ranger District of the George Washington and Jefferson National Forests. This out-of-the-way national forest stopover offers a great place to pitch a tent, whether you're here for a little trout fishing in local streams or part of the growing number of mountain bikers who have discovered this section of Craig County.

Pulling into the entrance off of VA 617, you'll find a campground divided into two loops, with the 17 sites well-spaced out among hardwoods and pines as the sites meander up the mountainside. There are no amenities to be found here, but the sites are as spacious as any I've seen in Virginia's national forests. Those looking for the most private sites will gravitate to the upper loop, which is not only farther from the road but away from the adjacent horse camping area as well. The overhead vegetation provides ample shade and a cool place to camp during the summer.

The Pines has been the staging site for the Escape mountain bike race—part of the East Coasters Virginia State Championship—for 13 years, making it the state's oldest race. Whether you're up to the task of taking on this challenging early autumn competition or just looking for some recreational riding, this area of the New Castle

CAMPGROUND RATINGS

Beauty: ★★★
Site privacy: ★★★★
Site spaciousness: ★★★★
Quiet: ★★★
Security: ★★
Cleanliness/upkeep: ★★★

There are no amenities to be found here, but the sites are as spacious as any to be found in Virginia's national forests.

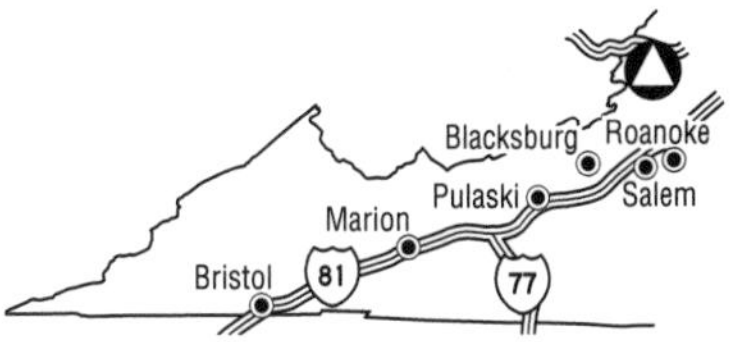

SOUTHWEST

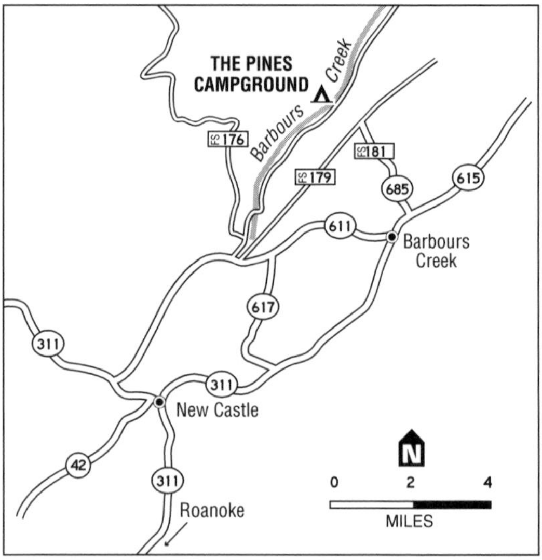

Ranger District may provide just what you're looking for. While Barbours Creek Wilderness is off-limits to cyclists, one can still pedal around this vast area on forest roads. In the course of researching *Mountain Bike! Virginia,* I was surprised to uncover a 25-mile abandoned railbed from New Castle to Oriskany that seemed unknown even to many of the Roanoke bikers. There are also a range of gravel Forest Service roads from which to choose.

Access to the Barbours Creek Wilderness is limited to the 2.3-mile Lipes Branch Trail, which runs from the Pines to FDR 5036 at the top of Potts Mountain. This is a strenuous hike, with an elevation gain of 2,000 feet. Should you take this route, you can plan to share the trail with equestrians utilizing the horse camp adjacent to the campground. However, there are a number of other area trails traversing Potts, Patterson, and Price Mountains. Heading back toward Roanoke, you can even access the Appalachian Trail along the North Mountain ridgeline, where VA 311 tops this ubiquitous mountain. Those looking for a less strenuous undertaking may want to plan a picnic at the nearby Fenwick Mines Recreation Area. Several nature trails traverse this biologically diverse area that once was home to a major iron ore and manufacturing complex. Hikers and mountain bikers should pick up a map of the New Castle District and trail brochures from the district's office for a better idea of what is available.

KEY INFORMATION

The Pines Campground
New Castle Ranger District
Box 246
New Castle, VA 24382

Operated by: U.S. Forest Service

Information: (540) 864-5195

Open: Year-round

Individual sites: 17

Each site has: Picnic table, fireplace, and lantern pole

Site assignment: First come, first served

Registration: On arrival

Facilities: Water and vault toilets

Parking: At campsite

Fee: None

Elevation: 1,840 feet

Restrictions:

Pets—On leash and attended

Fires—In camp stoves and fireplaces only; dead and down wood may be collected, no cutting or damaging live or standing dead trees

Alcoholic beverages—Permitted

Vehicles—Up to 16 feet

Other—Camp site should not be left unattended for a 24-hour period; quiet hours 10 p.m. to 6 a.m.

To get there: From I-81, take Exit141 onto VA 311 to New Castle. Turn right onto VA 615 and go 2 miles to VA 611. Turn left onto VA 611 and then turn right onto VA 617. Follow this for 5.5 miles to the Pines Campground.

CAVE SPRINGS RECREATION AREA

Dryden

Heading out to the far southwest corner of Virginia, you'll find an area known for coal production but largely overlooked by the rest of the state. Its topography of horizontal Appalachian Plateau sandstone identifies it more closely with that of neighboring Kentucky, Tennessee, and West Virginia. Those who live out here are known for their tenacity in carving out a life from a largely inhospitable landscape. Early timber and mining efforts denuded many of these mountains, and the Forest Service bought land for the Clinch Ranger District to protect the headwaters of the Tennessee River. I admit to having had as little exposure or interest in visiting far southwest Virginia as the next Virginian, but in the course of researching this book as well as *Mountain Bike! Virginia,* I was amazed by the natural beauty that lay in this obscure corner of the Old Dominion.

Cave Springs Recreation Area is one of those little-known gems harbored in Virginia's national forests. It lies at the foot of Stone Mountain, which is part of Cumberland Mountain, forming the border with Kentucky. Heck, most of us don't even know that our state shares a border with the Bluegrass State, but it does. While few Virginians may make the drive out to the Clinch Ranger District, those lucky enough to live nearby or in the neighboring states of Kentucky and Tennessee

CAMPGROUND RATINGS

Beauty:	★★★★
Site privacy:	★★★★
Site spaciousness:	★★★★★
Quiet:	★★★
Security:	★★★
Cleanliness/upkeep:	★★★

The quarter-acre spring-fed pond at Cave Springs is a great destination, especially during the heat of the summer.

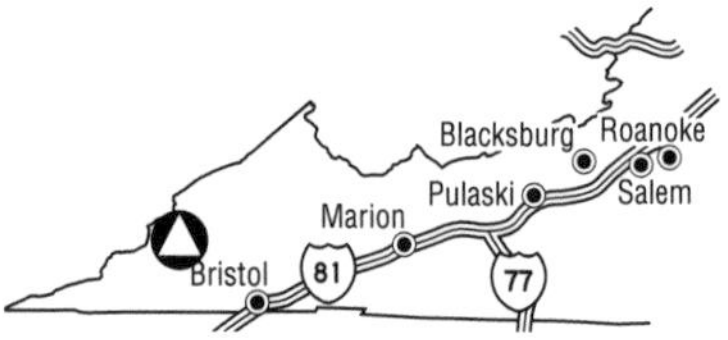

SOUTHWEST

can savor this outstanding camping destination.

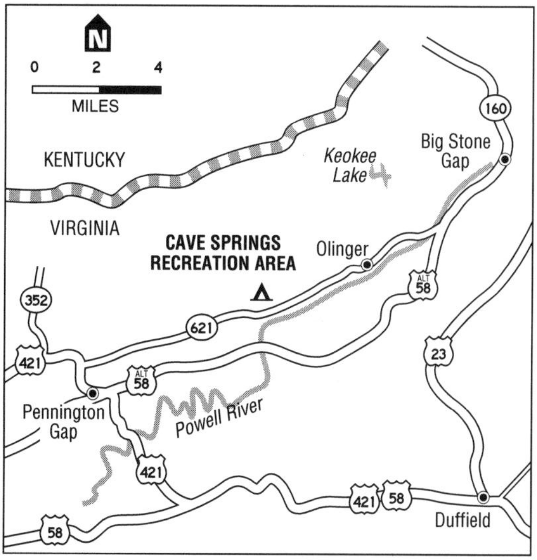

After passing through what is largely rolling agricultural landscape, you'll be surprised to find this wooded oasis with dense stands of holly hugging the quarter-acre spring-fed pond. Cave Springs is a great destination, especially during the heat of the summer. The entire recreation area is well-shaded under a canopy of hemlocks, and Recreation Specialist John Stallard says that the spring-fed pond stays below 72 degrees. So those looking to take a cool dip—a very cool dip—need look no farther. The campground's 41 sites are well-spaced along a single loop and very private, especially considering the area's low to moderate use. There's no need to recommend any particular sites, because all provide the private getaway that you'd expect from this campground—the farthest southwest of any in this guide. The narrow campground roads help minimize RV use as well. Native stone walls constructed by Forest Service employees and senior citizens in the 1960s permeate the area, along with wild rhododendron.

The one-mile Cave Overlook Trail loop will take you to the cave from which the area and spring derive their name. Spelunkers will be disappointed that the cave is not open to the public, but it's still a nice walk. Those hikers looking for a more strenuous outing can begin the 14.3-mile (point-to-point) Stone Mountain Trail at the Cave Springs Recreation Area. The cascading waters of Roaring Run and outstanding views of Virginia and Kentucky peaks make this trek well worth the effort. Along the way, you'll pass through old-growth hemlock that is more than 300 years old. A one-mile side-trip from Olinger

Gap will take you to Lake Keokee for some fishing or additional sightseeing.

The 92-acre Lake Keokee offers fishing for tiger muskie, largemouth bass, catfish, and sun fish, as well as limited picnicking facilities. Be sure to bring your canoe if you enjoy a quiet paddle around a lake with a number of interesting coves—gasoline motors are prohibited. Another option is to circle the lake on the fairly tame three-mile Lake Keokee loop trail.

Looking at the state's major population centers, it's safe to say that Cave Springs Recreation Area lies farther from most Virginians than any other destination you'll find in these pages. But don't let that stop you from putting aside the popular misconceptions regarding this region's socioeconomic status. Here is a beautiful land where you can find cool, quiet campgrounds when the rest of the state is basted by heat. Camp at Cave Springs, bask in the cool waters, hike the mountains, and discover all that's so refreshing about the part of Virginia that many Virginians have forgotten.

To get there: From Big Stone Gap, follow US 58A west for 3 miles to VA 621. Turn right onto VA 621 and follow it for 6.5 miles to the sign for Cave Springs.

KEY INFORMATION

Cave Springs Recreation Area
Clinch Ranger District
9416 Darden Drive
Wise, VA 24293

Operated by: U.S. Forest Service

Information: (540) 328-2931

Open: May 15–September 15

Individual sites: 41

Each site has: Picnic table and grill

Site assignment: First come, first served

Registration: On arrival

Facilities: Water, hot showers, and flush toilets

Parking: At campsite and small day-use area

Fee: $8 per night

Elevation: 1,380 feet

Restrictions:

Pets—On leash and attended

Fires—In camp stoves and fireplaces only; dead and down wood may be collected, no cutting or damaging live or standing dead trees

Alcoholic beverages—Public use prohibited

Vehicles—No limit

Other—Campsites should not be left unattended for a 24-hour period; quiet hours 10 p.m. to 6 a.m.

HURRICANE CAMPGROUND

Marion

If you're visiting the Mount Rogers National Recreation Area and want good access to the Iron Mountain, Appalachian, and Highlands Horse Trails, as well as close proximity to Mount Rogers—Virginia's highest point at 5,729 feet—then the Hurricane Campground may be just the place to pitch your tent. There is no shortage of campsites in the Mount Rogers area, and the nearby Beartree Recreation (73 sites) and Grindstone (92 sites) are large national forest campgrounds that attract many visitors to the area. Both of these are excellent campgrounds, but given a choice, wouldn't you rather pitch a tent next to Robert Frost at the campground less visited? I know I would.

Hurricane Campground is off VA 16, south of Marion with quite a few sites located along Hurricane Creek. After crossing the creek and entering the campground, you'll find that the first site on the right to be one of the best campsites anywhere. I certainly found that to be the case after traversing Virginia's campgrounds over the course of three decades. I've seen few places to camp that rival this setting—well off the campground road, out of sight from any other campsites, bordered by a pleasant stream, and nestled in the shade of towering hemlocks and rhododendrons. All of the campsites at Hurricane Campground offer more than a modicum of privacy and solitude. However, given individual tastes,

CAMPGROUND RATINGS

Beauty: ★★★★
Site privacy: ★★★★
Site spaciousness: ★★★★★
Quiet: ★★★★
Security: ★★★
Cleanliness/upkeep: ★★★

Few places rival this setting—well off the campground road, out of sight from any other campsites, bordered by a pleasant stream, and nestled in the shade of towering hemlocks and rhododendrons.

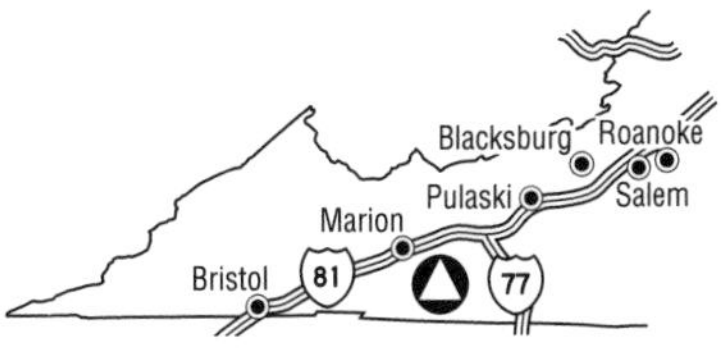

SOUTHWEST

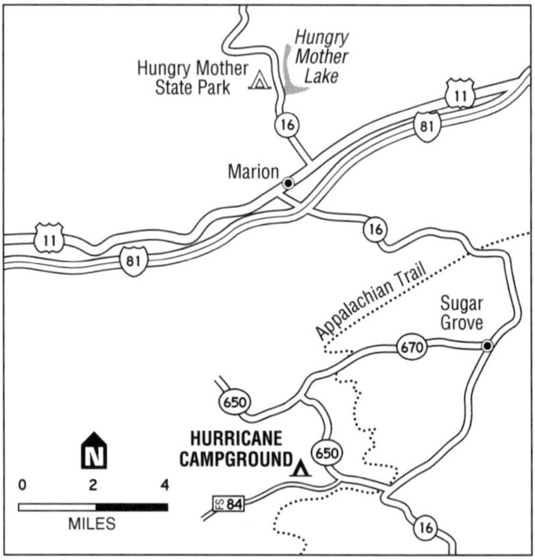

it's well worth looking around before picking a site and pitching your tent.

The paved campground continues straight, running parallel to the creek with sites 12, 18, 19, and 20 sitting right along its banks. Once you've reached site 20 on the right, the road curves to the left and winds uphill along the flank of Hurricane Knob. Sites 22–27 offer considerable seclusion and could be among your first choices, especially when the streams are overflowing their banks. Sites 26 and 27 are situated at the end of the campground loop and offer the additional benefit of limited drive-by traffic.

Unlike many national forest districts, the Mount Rogers National Recreation Area is managed for recreation. In addition to its relative seclusion, Hurricane Campground provides an excellent base camp from which to explore by foot, horse, or mountain bike some outstanding trails and forest roads.

The trailhead for the one-mile Hurricane Knob Loop Trail is located across from the information kiosk at the entrance to the campground. You can hike this moderate loop around the campground and up to Hurricane Knob as an after-dinner outing or a warm-up to some of the longer hiking possibilities that you'll find on over 400 miles of trails. The 9.6-mile Four Trails Circuit covers bits of the Dickey Gap, Comers Creek Falls, Iron Mountain, and Appalachian Trails as it winds its way through some of the Mount Rogers NRA's finest woodland scenery. For that matter, you can pick up a national forest map and plan to walk for a given distance on either the Iron Mountain or Appalachian Trail, both of which are fairly ubiquitous in this 115,000-acre recreation area.

Sixty miles of AT carve their way through the Mount Rogers area.

Although mountain bikes are not allowed on the Appalachian Trail, possibilities for two-wheel fun will seem limitless. Back when the sport was still trying to catch on in Virginia and other park agencies were not even acknowledging its existence, the folks at this district of the Jefferson National Forest were bold enough to proclaim that "whoever invented mountain bicycles surely had the Mount Rogers National Recreation Area in mind!" Those looking for minimal challenge and maximum fun will head for the 33-mile (one-way) Virginia Creeper Trail, a converted railroad bed that runs (downhill) from Whitetop Mountain to the town of Damascus. The Iron Mountain Trail gets a lot of use from local mountain bikers as well as visitors looking for additional technical and aerobic challenges. Combine a section (or more) of the Iron Mountain Trail with gravel forest development roads to create your own loop, or pick up one of the several guides that provide tried and true loop rides. The orange-blazed Virginia Highlands Horse Trail is also open to bikers, but be sure to yield right-of-way to equestrians when the occasion demands.

If trout fishing is your passion, then you need look no farther than Hurricane Creek or Comers Creek. As in other forms of outdoor play, you'll find angling opportunities abundant on over 100 miles of streams and two lakes within the area. Be sure to stop by the Mount Rogers ranger station on US 16 for a district map and trail brochures.

To get there: From I-81, go south on US 16. After entering the Mount Rogers NRA, turn right onto VA 650 and continue for 1.5 miles to FDR 84 and the entrance to the Hurricane Campground.

KEY INFORMATION

Hurricane Campground
Mount Rogers National Recreation Area
Route 1, Box 303
Marion, VA 24354

Operated by: U.S. Forest Service

Information: (540) 783-5196

Open: April–October

Individual sites: 27

Each site has: Picnic table, grill, and lantern pole

Site assignment: First come, first served

Registration: On site

Facilities: Pay telephone, flush toilets, and hot showers

Parking: At campsite

Fee: $12 per night

Elevation: 2,880 feet

Restrictions:

Pets—Must be on leash and attended

Fires—Use available grills

Alcoholic beverages—Prohibited

Vehicles—Up to 30 feet

Other—Length of stay no more than 14 days in a 30-day period; no cutting live trees; quiet time 10 p.m. to 6 a.m.

COMERS ROCK CAMPGROUND

Marion

With six campgrounds in the Mount Rogers National Recreation from which to choose, some might wonder why I'd choose the low-budget Comers Rock Campground for inclusion here. Its ten sites, vault toilets, and location away from the epicenter of outdoor activities in this 115,000-acre national forest recreation area will probably not draw many campers from the larger and spiffier campgrounds, such as Beartree and Grindstone; but in fact, those are the qualities that I felt made it suitable for sharing in a guide that offers camping alternatives that are farther from the "maddening" crowds.

Located a short distance from US 21 on the eastern end of the Mount Rogers NRA, this campground is located on gravel FDR 57. The views from this road running along the ridgeline of Iron Mountain are nothing short of spectacular. Iron Mountain forms a recreational as well as a geologic spine for the area with this campground situated in a saddle with northern views across the adjacent 2,858-acre Little Dry Run Wilderness. The campsites are arranged along a single loop with little vegetation between them; but they are well separated from each other with varied elevations to provide a modicum of privacy.

A trail next to the single toilet connects with the Virginia Highlands Horse Trail which meanders throughout Mount Rogers

CAMPGROUND RATINGS

Beauty: ★★★
Site privacy: ★★
Site spaciousness: ★★★
Quiet: ★★★
Security: ★★
Cleanliness/upkeep: ★★★

Iron Mountain forms a recreational as well as a geologic spine for the area with this campground situated in a saddle.

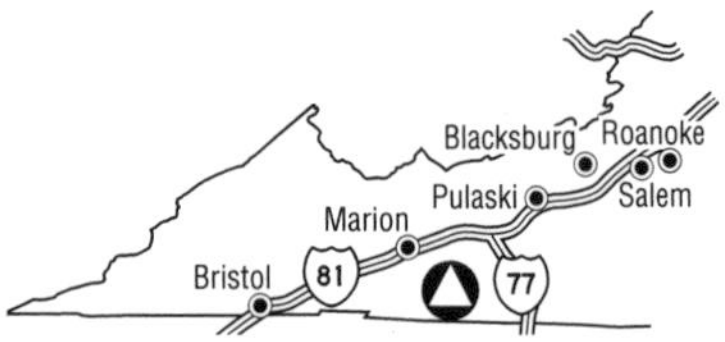

SOUTHWEST

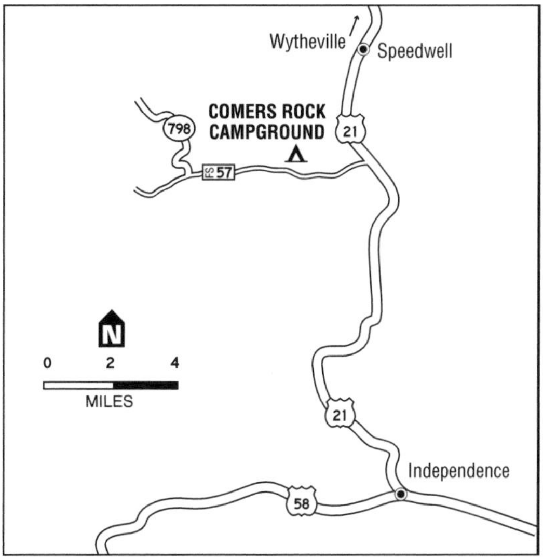

NRA along Iron Mountain. This is a multi-use trail, so hikers and mountain bikers can use the orange-blazed path to take off from their campsites for some outdoor exploration. However, given that bikes are not allowed in designated wilderness areas, it's best to begin pedaling west on the trail toward the five-acre Hale Lake, just two miles down the road. Those whose inclinations steer them away from single-track riding can start pedaling down FDR 57, which ends a short distance down the road just past the lake at the intersection with VA 672.

As the forest map for Mount Rogers states, "Whoever invented mountain bicycles surely had the Mount Rogers National Recreation Area in mind!"; and there is no shortage of places to ride in these parts. A close ride to Comers Rock Campground is one that I called "Mountain Bike Heaven" in *Mountain Bike! Virginia.* It's an eight-mile loop that's accessible from FDR 14 on the east side of US 21. You'll earn your aerobic stripes on the 2.6-mile climb but the 3-mile descent will have you clamoring for another go-round. Between the 33-mile Virginia Creeper Trail, and the vast network of forest roads and trails, opportunities for mountain biking here are abundant. Given its minimal amenities, you're more likely to use your site at Comers Rock Campground as a base from which to explore this 115,000-acre section of the George Washington and Jefferson National Forest.

However, mountain bikers are surely not the only ones who will appreciate the Mountain Rogers area. Equestrians will enjoy saddling up and taking in the sights along the Virginia Highlands Horse Trail, which stretches for 68 miles (point-to-point) from VA 94 near Ivanhoe to VA 600 at Elk Garden Gap. Trailer parking is available at the Hussy Mountain Horse Camp on FDR 14 along the previously-mentioned Mountain Bike Heaven loop through which the Highlands Horse Trail runs.

Hikers will also find ample places to get close to nature on more than 400 miles of trails that meander through this southwestern corner of the Old Dominion, including 60 miles of Appalachian Trail. The AT goes right through the town of Damascus. Whatever your outdoor interests, you're sure to find places to enjoy it at Mount Rogers.

To get there: From Wytheville, take US 21 through Speedwell and turn right onto FDR 57 at the top of Iron Mountain. Go 4 miles to the campground.

KEY INFORMATION

Comers Rock Campground
Mount Rogers National Recreation Area
Route 1, Box 303
Marion, VA 24354

Operated by: U.S. Forest Service

Information: (540) 783-5196

Open: Year-round

Individual sites: 10

Each site has: Picnic table, grill, and lantern pole

Site assignment: First come, first served

Registration: On-site

Facilities: Water and vault toilet

Parking: At campsite and picnic area

Fee: None

Elevation: 3,800 feet

Restrictions:

Pets—Must be on leash and attended

Fires—Use available grills

Alcoholic beverages—Prohibited

Vehicles—Up to 30 feet

Other—Length of stay no more than 14 days in a 30-day period; no cutting live trees

RAVEN CLIFF CAMPGROUND

Marion

Raven Cliff is the farthest from Mount Rogers of any of the seven campgrounds in the Mount Rogers National Recreation Area. Given its location and absence of amenities, most visitors to this 115,000-acre NRA will not be flocking to Raven Cliff. But their oversight is your gain. The agricultural land that surrounds the campground gives little indication as to the environmental niche that this campground occupies.

After initially passing through a flat, open area that is consistent with the rural surroundings, you'll enter a narrow ravine through which Cripple Creek (of the famed bluegrass tune) passes. The steep cliff lines the creek on one side while a grassy open area for equestrian campers is on the other. The free-flowing trout stream creates a beautiful scene as it courses through this gorge.

The campground loop is located uphill from the entrance road just across from the covered picnic pavilion. Turn left into the campground, and you'll find 20 sites (number 14/15 is a double site) tucked onto the side of Gleaves Knob under a canopy of pine, hemlock, and oaks. Sites 1 and 2 are located at the near end of the campground loop just outside the gated entrance, but those in search of maximum privacy should check the availability of sites 18–20 at the other end of the campground road. Site 20 is located on a small turnaround loop and is

CAMPGROUND RATINGS

Beauty: ★★★★
Site privacy: ★★★★
Site spaciousness: ★★★★★
Quiet: ★★★★★
Security: ★★★
Cleanliness/upkeep: ★★★

Given its location and absence of amenities, most visitors to this 115,000-acre NRA will not be flocking to Raven Cliff. But their oversight is your gain.

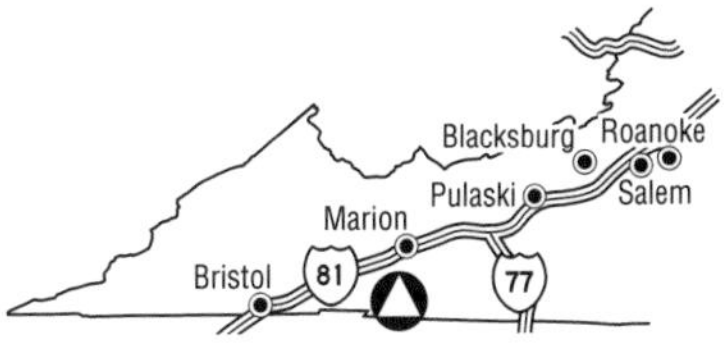

SOUTHWEST

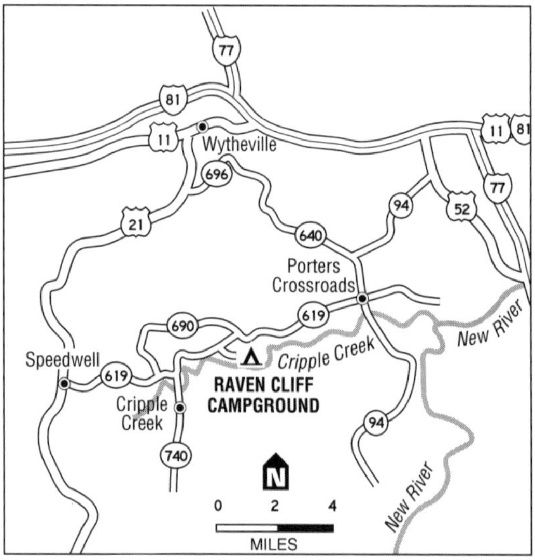

the most secluded of all. In short, this is a great little campground. Its out-and-back road past the 20 sites minimizes drive-through traffic, its out of the way location minimizes the number of campers, and its lush trees help keep things nice and quiet. If you don't mind driving a little to reach the Iron Mountain Trail, Appalachian Trail, Virginia Creeper Trail, and others in the Mount Rogers Recreation Area—or you're just looking for a great, secluded campground in which to pitch your tent—then Raven Cliff could be the place for your next camping trip.

Plan to take the one-mile (out-and-back) walk along Cripple Creek on the Raven Cliff Furnace Trail to see the remains of the furnace, in use until the early 1900s. Iron ore was mixed with limestone and charcoal and combined under extreme temperatures to form "pigs," which were then shipped to Richmond and other sites for casting.

After grousing about the distance to the various trails and recreational attractions that the Mount Rogers NRA has to offer, mountain bikers can enjoy some degree of comfort from Raven Cliff's relative proximity to the 57-mile New River State Park. Head south on VA 94, then turn left onto VA 602 to get onto the trail at the Byllesby Dam. The dam is near the southwestern prongs of the trail which end at Fries (pronounced "freeze") and Galax. Heading in a northeasterly direction on this converted railroad bed will also have you pedaling downhill for the better part of 30 miles toward the trail's northeastern terminus at Pulaski. The last 10 miles from Draper to Pulaski are on a slight uphill slope. In addition to largely avoiding vehicular traffic, one of the great advantages of rail-trail conversions such as the New River Trail is the modest gradient that you'll find. The downhills are enjoyable, and the uphills are very bearable.

Pedaling along this slight incline on the well-graded cinder surface is probably the easiest riding you're going to do. However, if you're planning an out-and-back and a 60-miler sounds a bit too ambitious, pedal from the Byllesby Dam at mile 37.3 to Shot Tower State Park at mile 25.2 along the New River Trail. This is a more manageable 24-mile round trip. In addition to safe and pleasant conditions on the trail, the scenery along this river—thought to be the oldest in North America—is pretty outstanding. Raven Cliff's proximity to the New River opens up all kinds of possibilities for paddlers and anglers too.

To get there: From Wytheville, take US 21 to the community of Speedwell. Turn left onto VA 619 and drive for 6.5 miles to the campground entrance on the right.

KEY INFORMATION

Raven Cliff Campground
Mount Rogers National Recreation Area
Route 1, Box 303
Marion, VA 24354

Operated by: U.S. Forest Service

Information: (540) 783-5196

Open: April–December 1 (Sites 1 & 2 are open year-round)

Individual sites: 25

Each site has: Picnic table, grill, and lantern pole

Site assignment: First come, first served

Registration: On site

Facilities: Flush toilet and water

Parking: At campsite and day-use area

Fee: $5 per night

Elevation: 2,240 feet

Restrictions:

Pets—Must be on leash and attended

Fires—Use camp stove or fire rings

Alcoholic beverages—Prohibited

Vehicles—Up to 30 feet

Other—Length of stay no more than 14 days in a 30-day period; no cutting live trees; quiet time 10 p.m. to 6 a.m.

HIGH KNOB RECREATION AREA

Norton

Perhaps I visited on an off-day (mid-week in July), but I found myself in the fortunate position of staying overnight at High Knob Recreation Area with my choice of all 14 sites and no other sounds than the ones Mother Nature intended to be there. With its small size, seclusion, absence of RV hookups, and small swimming hole located off by itself in the Clinch Ranger District of the George Washington and Jefferson Forest, this was one of those amazing finds that I made in the course of researching *The Best in Tent Camping: Virginia.* The log and stone construction at the High Knob Recreation Area was the handiwork of CCC workers in the 1930s.

After dropping down along the 1.7-mile driveway to reach the day-use area, I found the area to be lush with hemlocks, rhodendron, and an understory of ferns covering the moist ground while the rest of Virginia was suffering from a considerable draught. Just before the driveway's end on the right side of the road is the trail leading to the High Knob Observation Tower. At the bottom of the driveway is the parking lot for the day-use area and lake on the left with the campground entrance on the right. Because of the narrow twisty roads leading up to and into the campground, you're not likely to be rubbing elbows with RVers.

Located at an elevation of 3,800 feet, the four-acre "cold-water" spring-fed lake is guaranteed to provide a refreshing, if not

CAMPGROUND RATINGS

Beauty: ★★★★
Site privacy: ★★★★
Site spaciousness: ★★★★
Quiet: ★★★★★
Security: ★★★
Cleanliness/upkeep: ★★★★★

You'll want to make the 1.5-mile (one-way) assault on the observation tower at High Knob.

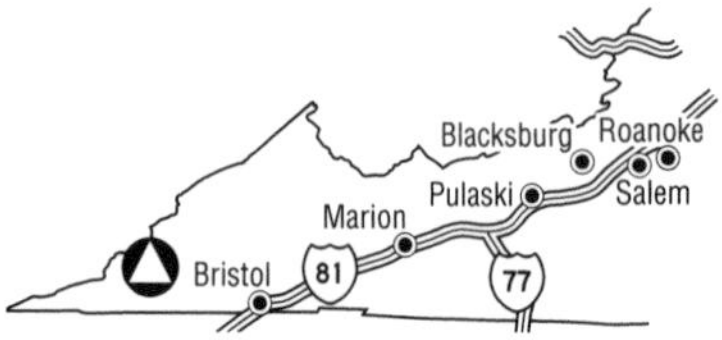

SOUTHWEST

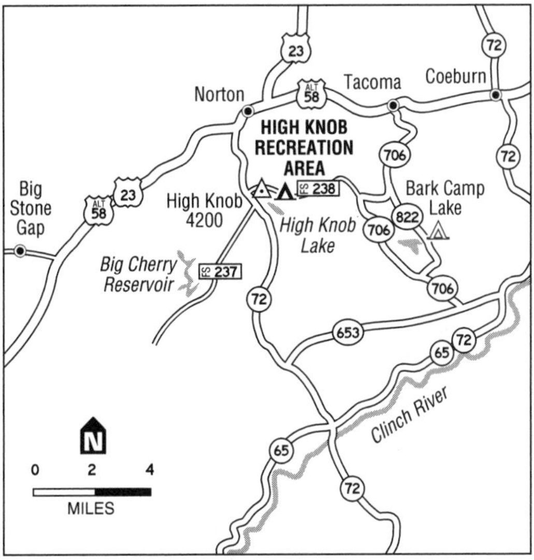

shocking wake-up call, or a pleasant dip on a hot, summer afternoon. In the absence of any noise from neighboring campsites, I opted to wake up on my own and stay bundled in my sleeping bag until 10 a.m., a real camping luxury. The ambient temperature at the campground was probably 20 degrees cooler than the rest of Virginia, which, at the time, was languishing under a 100-degree-plus daily heat wave. I was naturally curious about what the winters were like here, and campground host and lifelong local resident Lonnie Salyer regaled me with stories of 30- to 40-foot snow drifts as late as April—so much for four-season camping.

Aside from camping, picnicking, cool bathing, and enjoying the quiet, you'll want to make the 1.5-mile (one-way) assault on the observation tower at High Knob. At an elevation of 4,160 feet, the tower rises 400 feet above the campground and offers outstanding views of five states: Virginia, Kentucky, West Virginia, North Carolina, and Tennessee. This is one of the highest points in Virginia and makes a grat spot from which to observe the annual migration of birds of prey in the fall. Nonhikers can approach the tower by car via FDR 238 to enjoy this view.

The Observation Tower marks the beginning of the 18.7-mile (point-to-point) Chief Benge Scout Trail, which also wanders past Bark Lake Recreation Area before ending at the Little Stony National Recreation Trail. The Little Stony is a breathtaking 2.8 mile (one-way) trail that follows a former narrow-gauge railroad bed along Little Stony Creek via a 400-foot-deep gorge. Typical of former railroad beds, the Little Stony Trail retains less than a 4 percent grade. There is some good trout fishing along the Chief Benge Scout Trail, which was built as a joint venture between the Lonesome Pine District of the Boy Scouts and the Clinch Ranger District. Its length belies its level of difficulty, so don't try to cover the 18.7 miles unless you're a well-seasoned hiker. A more moderate day hike is the 10.5-mile one-way walk to Bark Camp Lake, which can be done with a shuttle at the end or as an introductory backpacking outing. Mountain bikers may want to test their mettle on the aforementioned trails, but most of us will enjoy pedaling along the myriad of open and gated forest development roads that lace the area. If you plan to do any exploration, be sure to pick up a copy of the Clinch Ranger District map from national forest headquarters in Wise.

To get there: From Norton, go 3.7 miles south on VA 619. Turn left onto FDR 238 and follow it for 1.6 miles to the campground entrance.

KEY INFORMATION

High Knob Recreation Area
Clinch Ranger District
9416 Darden Avenue
Wise, VA 24293

Operated by: U.S. Forest Service

Information: (703) 328-2931

Open: May 15–September 15

Individual sites: 14

Each site has: Tent pad, grill, picnic table, and lantern post.

Site assignment: First come, first served; no reservations

Registration: Self-registration on site

Facilities: Water and flush toilets

Parking: At campsites and day-use area

Fee: $8 per night

Elevation: 3,700 feet

Restrictions:

Pets—On leash only and not allowed in swimming areas

Fires—In fire rings, stoves, or grills only

Alcoholic beverages—Prohibited

Vehicles—Use only for entering or leaving, do not blocks roads or trails, and park in marked areas only

Other—Do not carve, chop, or damage any live trees; keep noise at a reasonable level

BARK CAMP LAKE

Coeburn

CAMPGROUND RATINGS

Beauty: ★★★★★
Site privacy: ★★★★
Site spaciousness: ★★★★
Quiet: ★★★★
Security: ★★★
Cleanliness/upkeep: ★★★

This is one of those campgrounds that has no bad sites.

The centerpiece of this out-of-the-way retreat located in the shadows of Stone Mountain is the 60-acre lake whose trout, bass, northern pike, catfish, and sunfish attract local anglers every day. One very distinguishing feature of this lake, however, is its three-mile irregular shoreline, which helps it blend naturally into this heavily wooded setting. Turning into the entrance for this recreation area, you'll descend for almost a mile before reaching the right turn for the campground. A short distance farther ahead on the main road is the picturesque waterfront picnic, boating, and fishing area.

The campground road winds around ravines heavily laden with wild rhododendron before reaching the new bathhouse and entrance to the two loops. On the left are sites with electric and water hookups, while the primitive tent sites are on the right. The tent sites are large and well spaced from one another with an additional buffer of oaks to provide shade and privacy. Sites 16, 17, and 18 are located at the end of the primitive loop and are the most secluded, but this is one of those campgrounds that has no bad sites. Those looking for a short walk can try the 0.5-mile Kitchen Rock Trail located at the end of the lakefront parking area. Hikers can also plan a 2.3-mile walk on the Lakeshore Trail, which is accessible from the end of the campground loop. The Lakeshore Trail

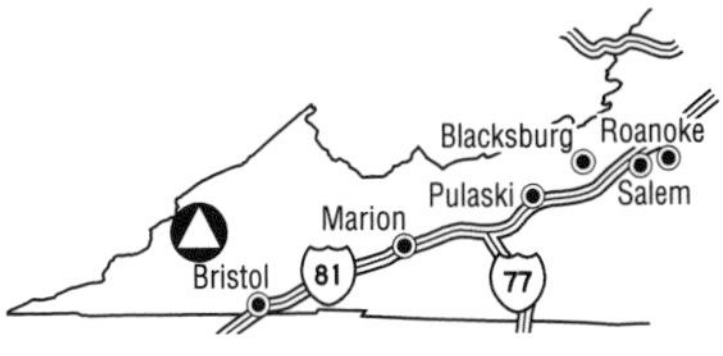

SOUTHWEST

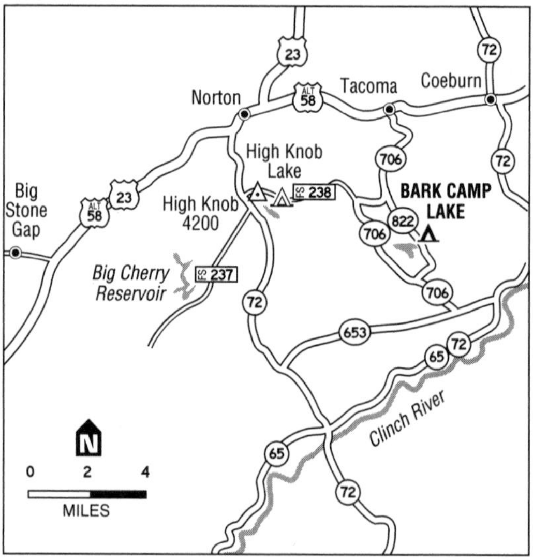

intersects with the 18.7-mile Chief Benge Scout Trail, a fairly strenuous outing that leads 9.6 miles northwest to High Knob and 6.8 miles southeast to the spectacular Little Stony National Recreation Trail. This 2.8-mile (point-to-point) trail offers an up-close look at Little Stony Creek as it rushes through a 400-foot rocky gorge complete with several waterfalls.

These and other trails are open to mountain bikers, although those in less than top-notch condition might want to limit their two-wheel travels to gated and open forest development roads. The Clinch Ranger District is tucked away in Virginia's southwest corner and offers numerous opportunities for outdoor adventure. Hiking trails, fishing lakes, and an endless combination of gated roads create a haven for outdoor lovers of all kinds. If you plan to do some exploring be sure to get a map of the district and have at it.

KEY INFORMATION

Bark Camp Lake
Clinch Ranger District
9416 Darden Drive
Wise, VA 24293

Operated by: U.S. Forest Service

Information: (540) 328-2931

Open: May 15–September 30

Individual sites: 19

Each site has: Picnic table, grill, and lantern pole

Site assignment: First come, first served

Registration: On site

Facilities: Water, flush toilets, and hot water showers

Parking: At campsite and extra parking in campground

Fee: $8 per night, $12 with electric hookup

Elevation: 2,780 feet

Restrictions:

Pets—Must be on leash and attended

Fires—Use camp stoves and available grills

Alcoholic beverages—May be consumed responsibly at campsite

Vehicles—Up to 30 feet

Other—Length of stay no more than 14 days in a 30-day period; no cutting live trees; quiet time 10 p.m. to 6 a.m.

To get there: From Norton, take US 58 east 6.3 miles to Tacoma, where you'll turn right onto VA 706. Follow 706 south for 4 miles and turn left onto VA 699. Turn right onto VA 822 and continue 1.7 miles to the entrance to the recreation area.

APPENDICES

APPENDIX A
Camping Equipment Checklist

Except for the large and bulky items on this list, I keep a plastic storage container full of the essentials of car camping so that they're ready to go when I am. I make a last-minute check of the inventory, resupply anything that's low or missing, and away I go!

Cooking Utensils
Bottle opener
Bottles of salt, pepper, spices, sugar, cooking oil, and maple syrup in waterproof, spill-proof containers
Can opener
Corkscrew
Cups, plastic or tin
Dish soap (biodegradable), sponge, and towel
Flatware
Food of your choice
Frying pan
Fuel for stove
Matches in waterproof container
Plates
Pocketknife
Pot with lid
Spatula
Stove
Tin foil
Wooden spoon

First Aid Kit
Band-Aids
First aid cream
Gauze pads
Ibuprofen or aspirin
Insect repellent
Moleskin
Snakebite kit
Sunscreen/chapstick
Tape, waterproof adhesive

Sleeping Gear
Pillow
Sleeping bag
Sleeping pad, inflatable or insulated
Tent with ground tarp and rainfly

Miscellaneous
Bath soap (biodegradable), washcloth, and towel
Camp chair
Candles
Cooler
Deck of cards
Fire starter
Flashlight with fresh batteries
Foul weather clothing
Paper towels
Plastic zip-top bags
Sunglasses
Toilet paper
Water bottle
Wool blanket

Optional
Barbecue grill
Binoculars
Books on bird, plant, and wildlife identification
Fishing rod and tackle
Hatchet
Lantern
Maps (road, topographic, trails, etc.)

APPENDIX B
Information

The following is a partial list of agencies, associations, and organizations to write or call for information on outdoor recreation opportunities in Virginia.

Blue Ridge Parkway
199 Hemphill Knob Road
Asheville, NC 28803
(828) 298-0398
www.nps.gov/blri

George Washington and Jefferson National Forests
5162 Valleypointe Parkway
Roanoke, VA 24019
(540) 265-5100
www.southernregion.fs.fed.us/gwj

Shenandoah National Park
3655 US Highway East
Luray, VA 22835
(540) 999-3500
www.nps.gov/shen

Virginia Department of Conservation and Recreation
203 Governor Street, Suite 213
Richmond, VA 23219
(800) 933-PARK
www.state.us/~dcr/parks

Virginia Department of Game and Inland Fisheries
4010 West Broad Street
Richmond, VA 23230
(804) 367-1000
www.dgif.state.va.us

APPENDIX C
Suggested Reading and Reference

Civil War Virginia: Battleground for a Nation. Robertson, James I. University Press of Virginia, 1993.

Day and Overnight Hikes in the Shenandoah National Park. Molloy, Johnny. Menasha Ridge Press, 1998.

A Guidebook to Virginia's Historical Markers. University Press of Virginia, 1989.

Highroad Guide to the Virginia Mountains. Winegar, Deane & Garvey. Longstreet Press, 1998.

Mountain Bike! Virginia. Porter, Randy Menasha Ridge Press, 1998.

Notes on the State of Virginia. Jefferson, Thomas. W.W. Norton & Company, 1982.

Roadside Geology of Virginia. Frye, Keith. Mountain Press Publishing Company, 1990.

Shenandoah National Park: An Interpretive Guide. Conners, James A. The McDonald & Woodward Publishing Company, 1988.

The Trails of Virginia. de Hart, Allen. University of North Carolina Press, 1995.

Virginia: A Guide to Backcountry Travel & Adventure. Bannon, James. Out There Press, 1997.

Virginia State Parks. Bailey, Bill. Glovebox Guidebooks of America, 1996.

INDEX

ABOUT THE AUTHOR

Randy Porter has been tromping around Virginia's nooks and crannies by foot, boat, and bicycle for the past 30 years. Degrees from the College of William and Mary and Virginia Commonwealth University led to a 20-year career teaching handicapped kids, from which he's now retired. Home for Randy is 120-some acres on the side of the Blue Ridge Mountains west of Charlottesville, just down the slope from Shenandoah National Park and the Appalachian Trail. His previous books include *A Cyclist's Guide to the Shenandoah Valley* and *Mountain Bike! Virginia.* He is currently at work on *60 Hikes Within 60 MIles: Richmond.*